REVIEWS OF NATIONAL POLICIES FOR EDUCATION

AUSTRIA

ORGANISATION FOR ECONOMIC CO-OPERATION AND DEVELOPMENT

ORGANISATION FOR ECONOMIC CO-OPERATION AND DEVELOPMENT

Pursuant to Article 1 of the Convention signed in Paris on 14th December 1960, and which came into force on 30th September 1961, the Organisation for Economic Co-operation and Development (OECD) shall promote policies designed:

— to achieve the highest sustainable economic growth and employment and a rising standard of living in Member countries, while maintaining financial stability, and thus to contribute to the development of the world economy;

— to contribute to sound economic expansion in Member as well as non-member countries in the process of economic development; and

— to contribute to the expansion of world trade on a multilateral, non-discriminatory basis in accordance with international obligations.

The original Member countries of the OECD are Austria, Belgium, Canada, Denmark, France, Germany, Greece, Iceland, Ireland, Italy, Luxembourg, the Netherlands, Norway, Portugal, Spain, Sweden, Switzerland, Turkey, the United Kingdom and the United States. The following countries became Members subsequently through accession at the dates indicated hereafter: Japan (28th April 1964), Finland (28th January 1969), Australia (7th June 1971), New Zealand (29th May 1973) and Mexico (18th May 1994). The Commission of the European Communities takes part in the work of the OECD (Article 13 of the OECD Convention).

Publié en français sous le titre :

EXAMENS DES POLITIQUES NATIONALES D'ÉDUCATION
AUTRICHE

Foreword

This is the fourth report on Austria in the long series of OECD *Reviews of National Policies for Education*. The first one dealt with the entire education system (published in 1968); the second one, with higher education and research (published in 1976); the third one with school policy (published in 1979).

The present report deals again with higher education and the issues its reform brings about. It is divided in two parts: the first reproduces a short version of the Background Report prepared for the review by the Austrian authorities, and the second one is the OECD Examiners' Report.

The examiners were Mr. de Larminat (France), Mr. Hochstrasser (Switzerland) and Mr. Pratt (United Kingdom).

This volume is published on the responsibility of the Secretary-General of the OECD.

Preface

Table of Contents

Part One

DIVERSIFICATION OF HIGHER EDUCATION IN AUSTRIA

Summary of the Background Report

Part Two
THE EXAMINERS' REPORT

The OECD Examiners

Mr. P. de LARMINAT
Inspection générale de l'administration de l'Éducation nationale – Paris (France)

Mr. U. HOCHSTRASSER
University of Bern (Switzerland)

Mr. J. PRATT (Rapporteur)
University of East London (United Kingdom)

The Austrian Delegation

Mr. Erhard BUSEK
Vice-chancelor and Federal Minister for Science and Research

Mr. Rudolf SCHOLTEN
Federal Minister for Education and Arts

Ministry of Education and Arts

Mr. Josef NEUMÜLLER — Director
Mr. Peter KREIML — Director
Mr. Ernst KOLLER — Secretary to the Minister
Mr. Christian BRÜNNER — Professor, University of Graz
Mr. Helmut SEEL — Professor, University of Graz

Ministry for Science and Research

Mrs. Eva KNOLLMAYER — Director
Mrs. Elsa GUNDACKER-HACKL — Deputy Director
Mr. Hans PECHAR — Deputy Director
Mr. Christian MÜLLER — Advisor to the Minister

Austrian Delegation to the OECD

Mrs. Ulrike MAGLOTH — *Ad interim* Permanent Representative
Mrs. Ulrike UNTERER — Scientific Attaché

Part One

DIVERSIFICATION OF HIGHER EDUCATION IN AUSTRIA

Summary of the Background Report

prepared by the Federal Ministry of Science and Research
and the Federal Ministry of Education and Arts
Vienna

Chapter 1

THE AUSTRIAN EDUCATION SYSTEM

General features of the education system

Education in Austria is considered a public service at all levels. The private sector is small by size and significance, and in some cases, such as university, does not exist at all. Only in preschool education on the one hand, and vocational and continuing education on the other does the private sector play an important role.

The majority of schools and all universities are public institutions. Schools are owned by the Federal State or the Provinces (*Länder*), while universities are owned by the Federal State. Decision-making power is concentrated at the top of the system, held either by the Federal State or the Provinces. Leadership at the top of the institutions, whether schools or universities, is comparatively weak, which contributes to a high degree of uniformity and equity with very little institutional differences: all institutions of the same type are supposed to have the same standards and reputation and confer the same credentials.

The post-war period in industrialised countries was characterised by an impressive expansion of prestigious and demanding educational provisions which had been previously reserved to a small elite. In Austria, this development started in the 1960s but expansion remained below OECD average. One characteristic of the Austrian situation is that the expansion of student numbers did not go hand in hand with a structural reform of the education system. Neither did Austria follow the course of most industrialised countries in adopting a comprehensive system at the lower secondary level, nor did it adopt the strategy of diversifying the post-secondary sector as a response to expansion. Consequently the expansion of the education system took place within the structure of an outdated elite system which had to cope with continuously growing numbers of students.

Outline of the school system

General characteristics and legal foundations

Austria, like other German-speaking countries, has not established a comprehensive system at the lower secondary level. As a consequence, student streams separate at the early age of 10. A (continuously growing) minority of pupils enter the *Gymnasium* (AHS), the elite track of secondary school, which prepares students for higher education. The majority enter the *Hauptschule,* or four-year secondary school leading to the apprenticeship system. The problem caused by the existence of different tracks at the lower secondary level is one of the most controversial issues in Austrian education policy. For more than two decades the Social Democratic Party has made attempts to create a comprehensive school but these attempts failed due to the fact that major changes in the school system require broad political consensus (*i.e.* a two-third majority in Parliament).

Another feature of the Austrian school system is the relatively early age – by OECD standards – at which young people enter vocational training. Indeed, the majority of youngsters enter the apprenticeship system at the age of 15. However, the more demanding schools of vocational education and training (*berufsbildende höhere Schulen* – BHS) also start at this age. In the 1960s, some upper secondary vocational courses (especially the training of teachers for compulsory schools) were upgraded to the post-secondary level while training for engineering and for commercial careers remained at secondary level.

Teachers are, for the most part, civil servants; by international standards, their wages and reputation are satisfactory. However, there is a strong division within the teaching profession: teachers of compulsory schools are trained in non-university courses, while teachers for the upper secondary general or vocational schools have a university degree. Not only is there a difference in the wages and the reputation of those groups, they also represent two different educational cultures.

An important characteristic of the Austrian school system is its structural inertia. This is partly due to the general nature of huge bureaucratic organisations but also has a more specific basis in the legal foundations. The passing of new acts as well as the amendment of old school acts require a two-third majority in Parliament. Responsibility for school acts was not embodied in the Constitution until 1962 because of mutual mistrust of the Conservative and the Social Democratic Parties. The necessity of attaining a broad consensus in Parliament seems to be an obstacle to education reform.

Legal authority and responsibility in the actual school system is characterised by a complex balance of power. Four different categories may be distinguished:

- federal responsibilities in both legislation and administration;
- federal responsibilities in legislation, provincial responsibilities in administration;
- federal responsibilities in basic legislation, provincial responsibilities in implementing legislation and administration;
- provincial responsibilities in both legislation and administration.

Federal responsibilities are safeguarded by the Federal Ministry of Education. Provincial responsibilities are safeguarded by a Provincial School Board, which is composed according to the strength of political parties as determined by the results of the most recent election in the province.

As a matter of principle, anyone can start a private school in Austria. There are several types, which are enumerated below by ascending privileges and, collaterally, by possibility of State intervention:

- enterprises which, for lack of a moral-education component, are not schools as defined by school law (*e.g.* driving and dancing schools);
- schools enjoying no public privileges which must only comply with safety regulations, etc.; attending them does not fulfil the obligation of compulsory schooling;
- schools declared suitable by the Federal Ministry for fulfilling the obligation of compulsory schooling but not empowered to issue public certificates;
- "accredited" schools, which are empowered to issue public certificates;
- schools labeled by a name listed in the School Organisation Act (SchOG) – these institutions must comply with all regulations that public schools are subject to, with the exception of open admission and absence of tuition fees.

The last two types of private schools may be awarded public subsidies, unless they are profit-oriented. In some cases, such as schools maintained by churches and denominations, federal authorities pay teachers' salaries.

Structure

Schools for 6- to 14-year-olds

- *Primary school (Volksschule*; ages 6 through 10)

Primary school covers grades 1 through 4; its task is to impart a common elementary education to children, *i.e.* balanced basic schooling of the social, emotional, intellectual and physical facets of their personalities. Handicapped children are integrated into regular schools if possible. There are ten subtypes of Austrian special schools for pupils whose integration is impossible (ages 6 to 15).

In grade 4 parents are informed about educational career options for the following year, and teachers formulate recommendations on the basis of pupils' interests and achievements.

- *Compulsory secondary school (Hauptschule*; ages 10 to 14)

The only prerequisite for admission to compulsory secondary school is successful completion of grade 4 of primary school. Subject teachers are provided. After an observation period (3 weeks to 1 semester), pupils are assigned to one of three ability groups in German, mathematics and a modern language, the requirements of each top achievement group being the same as in the secondary general school (AHS). Pupils showing above-average achievement in compulsory secondary school may transfer to the secondary general school.

- *Lower secondary general school (AHS,* ages 10 to 14)

Traditionally, this type of school (*Gymnasium*) prepares students for higher education. It consists of a lower and an upper level, the final examination of the upper level cycle giving access to higher education. Instruction is given by subject teachers.

There are several types of specialisation within lower secondary general school (grades 5 through 8):

- First and second years: identical syllabus for all; one modern language.
- Third and fourth years: *Gymnasium*: Latin; *Realgymnasium*: geometric drawing, extra mathematics; *wirtschaftskundliches Realgymnasium*: extra chemistry and handicraft.

Students from compulsory secondary school or comprehensive school are admitted to upper secondary general school at the end of a school year on the basis of excellent achievement; otherwise, they must pass an admission test in selected subjects.

Schools for 14- to 19-year-olds

After lower secondary school students have a variety of choices: they may go on to a full-time education in upper secondary school, either general (AHS) or vocational (BHS, BMS); they may begin an apprenticeship combining practical training in an enterprise with attendance at part-time vocational school ("dual system"); or may leave the education system. Since compulsory school ends at the age of fifteen, students who begin an apprenticeship and those who want to leave the education system must attend pre-vocational school.

- *Pre-vocational school* (ages 14 to 15)

This type of school offers extended general education as well as basic education for practical life and for the world of work, together with vocational orientation in preparation of a choice of career.

- *Upper secondary general school (AHS, ages 14 through 18)*

Students are normally promoted from lower secondary general school to upper secondary general school on the basis of continuous assessment of a year's work. The following subtypes are provided; they differ only in the compulsory subjects specified:

- *Gymnasium*: classical branch with Latin; also Greek or a second modern language;
- *Realgymnasium*: extra mathematics; also Latin or a second modern language; descriptive geometry or extra biology and environmental science, chemistry, physics;
- *Wirtschaftskundliches Realgymnasium*: second modern language or Latin; nutrition and home economics; extra geography and economics, biology and environmental science, psychology, education and philosophy;
- *Oberstufenrealgymnasium* (grades 9 to 12 only, transfer from other schools after grade 8): second modern language or Latin; instrumental music or handicraft or descriptive geometry or extra biology and environmental science, chemistry, physics (and mathematics).

- *Part-time vocational schools* (ages 15 to 19, "dual system")

Approximately half of all 15-year-olds are apprentices; they attain skilled-worker level in a regulated "apprenticeable trade" after two to four years, depending on the trade concerned. They are paid apprentices' wages subject to collective bargaining as they contribute to the enterprise. Besides their training in an enterprise on a contractual basis, they are subject to compulsory vocational schooling irrespective of age and thus attend part-time vocational schools during 20 to 30 per cent of the curriculum on the basis of day release (1 to 1½ days per week) or block release (8 to 12 weeks per year), depending on the trade and geographical considerations. Enterprise-based training culminates in a final examination, the theoretical portion of which is waived if the apprentice has successfully completed the part-time vocational school.

- *Full-time vocational schools (BMS,* ages 14 to 18)

These schools also lead up to skilled-worker level; however, a high proportion of general education usually qualifies graduates for jobs at a slightly higher level. Most full-time vocational curricula are of three or four years' duration. However, there are also some one-year and two-year types, usually requiring no entrance examination and offering only semi-skilled training.

There are full-time vocational schools in the following fields:

- industry and trade, *e.g.* metalwork, electricity, electronics, building, chemistry, textiles and fashion, wood, glass, graphic trades, hotels and catering, crafts (3 or 4 years);
- commerce (1, 2 or 3 years);
- "economics": combined training in domestic science and commerce and in some areas of the hotel and catering trades (1, 2 or 3 years);
- social work (no entrance examination) and nursing (1, 2, 3 or 4 years);
- agriculture and forestry (no entrance examination; 1, 2, 3 or 4 years).

- *Upper secondary vocational schools (BHS,* ages 14 to 19)

These schools offer training for a period of five years leading up to engineering-technician or middle-management level. This form of education exists essentially in the same fields as full-time vocational programmes. The only exceptions are social work and paramedical occupations, for which post-secondary training is provided. In addition, a few higher secondary vocational schools cater mainly or exclusively to handicapped pupils.

Enrolment figures at upper secondary vocational schools have increased dramatically over the last twenty years in both absolute and relative terms; more students have already graduated from these institutions than from upper secondary general schools, and the former are currently enrolling in university at a rate of 44 per cent.

- *Schools for kindergarden teachers and educators* (ages 14 to 19)

Nursery school teachers[1] and teaching staff in boarding schools, etc., are also trained over five years, in schools to which most of the characteristics mentioned above also apply. Graduates of either subtype may add a two-year course qualifying them for dealing with handicapped children.

Second-chance education

The graduation qualifications of upper secondary general schools as well as of full-time vocational (upper secondary vocational/technical) schools can also be attained at a later date by persons who have successfully completed grade 8 or acquired some further qualification. Courses which broaden or deepen previously acquired vocational qualifications are available. These schools may offer day or evening classes for employed persons, the latter with an extended duration.

Outline of the higher education system

General characteristics and legal foundations

Austria is one of the few countries which has not established non-university alternatives in the course of the expansion of higher education. The first steps to establish a non-university sector (NUS) were undertaken in the mid-1960s, when the training of teachers for compulsory schools was upgraded and teacher training academies were founded. However, plans to upgrade the training of engineers and to enlarge the non-university sector were rejected at the end of the 1960s. The NUS remained small and has even lost importance in the last fifteen years.

The NUS is marginal not only in a quantitative sense. From an Austrian point of view, neither the academies for teacher training or social workers nor the medico-technical schools are part of the higher education system. Higher education in Austria is regarded as a monopoly of research universities. The strong borderlines between the university sector and the NUS are reflected in the fact that there is no permeability between the two sectors.

The school-like organisation of the NUS as opposed to the greater autonomy of the universities is reflected by the fact that these institutions are regulated in the Act on School Organisation. Therefore there is also an administrative separation. The Minister for Education and Arts, rather than the Minister for Science and Research, has the political and administrative responsibility for the NUS.

Despite the large academic autonomy (in the sense of freedom for teaching and research) Austrian universities have little institutional autonomy. They are state-owned and mainly state-run institutions, not corporate bodies with a legal identity. There is a sphere of autonomous administration which, however, is basically restricted to the right to pass resolutions on proposals to be forwarded to the Minister for Science and Research, who then takes the decision. Responsibility for the university sector is carried by the federal State, the provinces having no authority in this matter. Universities are almost exclusively financed by public funds, the money being distributed by line budgets and university staff being mainly civil servants.

Because decision-making power is concentrated at the top of the system, *i.e.* in the Federal Ministry of Science and Research, authority at institution level is comparatively weak. The Rector at the head of each institution does not carry the power required for efficient university management either externally (with respect to State administration) or internally (with respect to the internal centres of power at universities). The Rector's task is rather to represent his or her university.

The non-university sector (NUS)

Colleges of social work

In 1991/92 a total of 998 students were enrolled in the nine colleges of social work. Unlike the university sector, which is owned by the federal State, some of these institutions are owned and run by the provinces or by non-governmental organisations. Besides their regular courses some of these three-year colleges also offer evening classes for employed persons. Graduates of vocational schools of social work are admitted without a higher secondary school final examination (*Matura*); they must, however, first attend a preparatory class.

Teacher training colleges for general education

There are fourteen institutions of this type, including eight public ones, the others being run by the Roman Catholic Church. In 1991/92 a total of 5 486 students were enrolled in teacher training colleges for general education. These colleges comprise three-year courses for teachers at:
- primary schools;
- compulsory secondary schools;
- special schools;
- pre-vocational schools.

Preparatory classes exist for students who did not pass an upper secondary school final examination. There are practice schools attached to each college.

Teacher training colleges for vocational education

There are twelve institutions of this type, including seven institutions for religious instruction which are owned by the Church. In 1991/92 a total of 1 295 students were enrolled in these colleges which comprise teacher training courses for:
- part-time vocational schools (2 years; reduced to 1 year after 2 years of teaching, accompanied by a course at a Further Teacher Training Institute);

- workshop instruction at full-time vocational and higher secondary vocational schools as well as theoretical technical instruction at full-time vocational schools (*ditto*);
- home-economics instruction (2 to 3 years);
- word-processing (including shorthand and typing, 2 years);
- full-time and part-time vocational schools of agriculture and forestry (2 years);
- upper secondary vocational schools of agriculture and forestry ($\frac{1}{2}$ year after a university degree).

Again, there are practice schools; vocational practice is also imparted in companies and several years' industrial practice is required in addition to the upper secondary school final examination. In most courses the final examination can be waived for master craftsmen with extended industrial practice.

Medico-technical schools

There are 33 institutions of this kind and seven types of specialisation in medico-technical occupations. They are based in hospitals. In 1991/92 a total of 1 854 students were enrolled in these schools, which are owned and run by the owners of the hospitals.

The university sector

Organisational structure

There are three levels of responsibility within the university sector, each of which is represented by a board and an individual:
- The whole university is represented by the Rector and the University Board. The Rector, a tenured professor, is elected for a two-year term by a university assembly comprising representatives from all university staff groups. The Rector's functions are to implement the decisions of the University Board and its commissions, to supervise current affairs and to represent the university to the outside world. The University Board deals with delegated federal matters pertaining to the whole university; as far as autonomous matters are concerned it is responsible for co-ordination and supervision of the smaller units and lower-level authorities.
- At the level of the faculty, management functions are performed by the Faculty Board and the Dean. The Dean, a tenured professor, is elected for a period of two years by the faculty committee comprising all the faculty professors but also representatives of assistants and other staff as well as students. The Dean's functions comprise representation to the outside world, current business and implementation of the Board's decisions. The responsibilities of both the Dean and the Faculty Board are, however, limited to the institutes and units attached to the faculty which applies to matters of instruction and research as well as to administrative matters. In universities without faculties, the University Board takes over the tasks of the Faculty Boards.

– Each institute is headed by a professor, who is elected by the Institute Conference, comprising equal numbers of professors, lecturers/assistants and students. A Study Board is established for each curriculum with the main task of overseeing a study plan.

Curricula

The basis of curricular regulations is the General University Studies Act (*allgemeines Hochschulstudiengesetz*), which came into force in 1966. Regulations contained in this act establish guidelines for enrolment, registration, curricular structure and organisation, types and details of examinations, as well as the conferring and legal protection of academic degrees.

In parallel to this fundamental act, there are special University Studies Acts applying to individual curricula or to groups of curricula. They regulate such matters as the naming of curricula, their subdivision into specialisations, the duration of studies, the subjects of examinations for the Master's and Doctor's degrees, and the wording of academic degrees and related titles.

Beyond these general and specific acts of Parliament, there are the curricula established by an ordinance of the Federal Ministry of Science and Research. The Ministry prescribes which curricula shall be taught at a given university, what classes shall be compulsory or optional within a curriculum, the number of hours assigned to them, and what subjects the examinations shall comprise. On the basis of these curricula, the Study Boards of individual universities decide on their study plans.

The most common type of university curricula are the regular curricula which include Master's degree curricula, doctoral curricula, short curricula, the M.D. curriculum, and upgrading curricula and applie to approximately 96 per cent of the student population.

With the exception of medicine, doctoral studies can only be undertaken subsequent to completion of a Master's degree curriculum. The latter is usually divided into two cycles, each of which terminates with a formal examination. In addition, a thesis must be submitted for graduation. Certain Master's degree curricula require a combination of two disciplines.

The minimum duration of Master's degree curricula is eight or nine semesters. However, only exceptional students tend to successfully complete their studies within this period. The minimum duration of doctoral curricula is two semesters which culminate in a dissertation and a doctoral examination in several subjects.

New Master's degree curricula can be established on a provisional basis for a limited period. After the trial period has elapsed, the Federal Ministry of Science and Research decides whether the provisional curriculum is awarded regular status.

There are also alternatives to the regular types of Master's degree studies. Students may apply to the Federal Ministry of Science and Research for the permission to follow an individualised curriculum (*Studium irregulare*). In order to supplement Master's degrees, graduates may engage in extension studies. While these feature final examinations, no academic degrees or comparable titles are awarded. Similar rules apply to the short curricula, which currently exist for translators, data-processing specialists and actuaries. Besides these regular curricula there are also non-degree university courses, the purpose of which is either further training of graduates or specialised vocational education. However, these are not particularly attractive to students because they confer neither academic degrees nor vocational privileges.

Students

Owing to the lack of non-university alternatives, most entrants to higher education choose university studies. In 1991/92 a total of 177 000 Austrian students were enrolled in the university sector. Even though the number of university entrants is currently stagnating and may even decrease in the future, little short-term change is expected in the overcrowding of universities. Total enrolment is still increasing, though at a slower rate: while Austrian student enrolment increased by approximately 13 per cent between 1969 and 1979, the corresponding figure for the following decade is only 7.5 per cent.

Approximately one-third of Austrian students are enrolled in the University of Vienna, the runners-up being the Universities of Graz and Innsbruck. The fastest growth rates, however, are shown by the Technical Universities in Vienna (+23.6 per cent between the winter semesters of 1986/87 and 1989/90) and Graz (+21.4 per cent). The runner-up is the University of Economics in Vienna with a growth rate of approximately 18 per cent. The traditional universities, by way of contrast, only show below-average growth rates.

It is worth noting that the average age of students is rising. At present, the proportion of students older than 25 years is approximately 35 per cent, whereas in the early 1980s this only amounted to 25 per cent.

The social background of students, on the other hand, shows only minor shifts. In the 1988/89 winter semester, approximately 19.5 per cent of the student population was found to have a self-employed father, 66 per cent a white-collar father and 13 per cent a blue-collar father.

A regional survey of university entrants shows that enrolment for students from Vienna doubled between the winter semesters of 1970/71 and 1989/90, well below the Austrian average growth rate of 138 per cent. In Styria and the Burgenland the increase of new enrolments also remained well below the national average. Above-average increases, on the other hand, were noted in the Provinces of Lower Austria (+205 per cent) and Vorarlberg (+195 per cent).

While the proportion of university graduates is increasing, their chances of obtaining a job corresponding to their qualifications are rapidly deteriorating. One of the consequences of this situation is that many recent university graduates begin their professional careers in temporary or part-time jobs and expect corresponding fluctuations of their income.

University staff

The staff of universities and colleges of art and music is divided into two main categories: scientific/scholarly/artistic staff on the one hand and administrative staff on the other. The first category is mainly made up of teachers not all of whom, however, are tenured civil servants; some are employed on a part-time basis.

The term "university teacher" comprises not only professors, but the teaching staff as a whole (professors emeriti, assistants, non-employed lecturers and honorary professors).

This wide range of functions is reflected in the conditions of appointment: in general, no formal teaching qualification is legally required for university teachers. Teaching and research privileges are acquired with an appointment and terminate together with it. The only exception is "Habilitation", which entails teaching privileges even without an appointment.

The teaching privileges of assistants are formally restricted to an auxiliary function but the expansion of universities has made this a dead letter since 40 per cent of all university classes are currently being held by assistants.

While all professors are tenured civil servants, assistants are normally non-tenured civil servants. Some of them are employed by the university and paid with money from research contracts. University teachers entrusted for a given period or permanently with conducting individual classes (guest professors, honorary professors, lecturers, instructors) are not civil servants.

Chapter 2

THE DISCUSSION ON THE REFORM
OF THE AUSTRIAN HIGHER EDUCATION

There has been growing dissatisfaction with the Austrian education system since the late 1980s. Currently, there is a widespread view that educational expansion has gone too far and too quickly. Only for a very brief period in the 1960s was there a broad consensus on the fact that the economy would need more graduates from upper secondary schools and universities. At the time, all political groups agreed on a policy of modernisation and expansion of the education system but this consensus ended in the late 1960s. Ever since, the issue of educational expansion has been highly controversial.

The fact that more and more students enter upper secondary school is regarded, especially by the business community, as a tendency towards overeducation which will result in a lack of qualified blue-collar workers. There was significant resistance against the growth of university-student numbers from the academic community, which was supported partly by the conservatives and by the business community. Thus, in most cases the term ''mass university'' is not used in a descriptive, but in a disparaging way.

The great uniformity in the education system was considered as preponderantly advantageous for a long time:

- as long as there was confidence in planning as a means of molding social processes, the State monopoly could be considered the expression of a higher social rationality;
- the centralisation of decision structures facilitates the creation of equal conditions for all groups of the population;
- in a democracy, State control of educational institutions guarantees that the interests of all groups within the education system are taken into account; functionalising the education system in support of the interests of a minority to the detriment of the majority seems to be out of the question.

Recently, the discussion on education policy in Austria gradually concentrated on the disadvantages of a high degree of uniformity:

- the necessity to reach a consensus on every single issue leads to immobility and low adaptability;

– the high degree of centralisation of decisions leads to diminished influence for those most concerned;
– the compromise nature of most decisions means that hardly anybody can truly endorse them.

The debate on school autonomy

School autonomy is a new issue in the public discussion of Austrian education. It was brought up for the first time in 1988. Several strands in this debate may be distinguished:

– One strand links autonomy with the introduction of more competition and market-orientation into the education system. From this point of view the high degree of regulation and bureaucratisation shields schools from clients' demands, making them highly resistant to change. Autonomy is supposed to bring more external pressure on the education system which would lead to more efficiency, flexibility, and orientation towards clients.
– Another strand emphasizes the democratisation of the school system. School autonomy is supposed both to give more say to teachers, students and parents, and to increase the impact of democratic values in classroom work. Teachers in particular hope that autonomy will simplify the administrative superstructure and involve them more directly in decision-making. There is also the expectation that school autonomy will reduce the influence of political parties on the education system.
– School autonomy was also welcomed by various educational grass roots initiatives. From the late 1970s onwards teachers and parents formed groups which wanted to pursue "school development from the grass roots" in local settings.
– Finally, there is a tendency, especially within the political establishment of the provinces, to emphasize school autonomy in terms of regionalisation. Since the problems of the lower secondary school are obviously not solvable on a federal level, some regional education authorities argue for more room for manœuvre to find regional and local solutions.

The Ministry of Education and Arts has tried to promote public discussion on school autonomy since 1991. An expert opinion has been commissioned, public hearings have been organised, decision-making power over local budgets has been devolved to some schools on an experimental basis and an amendment to the School Organisation Act (SchOG) has been prepared. The amendment gives schools the power to take decisions at the local level concerning parts of the curriculum and some matters of time organisation.

However, after a short period of euphoria, this move towards autonomy has been increasingly criticised. Some teachers, particularly representatives of the unions, argue that autonomy in a period of financial constraints could result in devolving the "administration of shortage" to schools.

The debate on organisational reform of universities

In the fall of 1991 the Ministry proposed a reform with the intention of effecting fundamental change in the Austrian tradition of governance and administration of universities. This so-called "Green Paper" included a remarkable degree of institutional autonomy and proposed, on many crucial points, to transfer decision-making power from the Ministry to the universities. This was based on the condition that managerial bodies within the universities would have to be created – bodies to which the decision-making power could be shifted. Most important was the proposal to institute change at the head of the institution. In other words, the Rector who is elected by the faculties would be replaced by a President appointed by the Minister.

This Green Paper was severely criticised by all groups within the university. It was revised by an expert group and the Minister presented the so-called "Orange Paper" half a year later. This new proposal still faces fundamental criticism. However, the Minister has made it clear that he has decided to realise the basic concepts of the proposal. What are these basic concepts?

An important innovation will be the creation of a buffer organisation, the *Universitäten-Kuratorium,* which will have the task of system-wide co-ordination. The most divisive point is still the reorganisation of the internal governance structures of the university. The concept of the Orange Paper is that there should be a division of functions and power at all organisational levels, *i.e.* at the level of the institute, of the faculty and of the institution as a whole. On the one hand, there will be a strategic body responsible for taking decisions concerning the fundamental directions of an institution and for controlling the executive body. This executive body, on the other hand, will have the authority to realise the strategic plans.

The constitution of both bodies mirrors their different functions. The strategic body is elected by different groups within the university. The executive body is also elected, but by a highly selected group which can be influenced by the superior body. At present, universities are not headed by a president but by a rector and three or more vice-rectors. However, this rector has basically the same functions as the president described in the Green Paper. The main difference is that the influence of the Minister on the appointment is currently rather limited.

The strengthening of managerial structures makes it possible to shift significant decision-making power from the Ministry to the buffer organisation and to the single universities. The authority of the Ministry is now limited to the task of determining the global goals and a framework for the overall system. The buffer organisation has the task of system-wide co-ordination and allocation of lump-sum budgets to the single institutions. It is the responsibility of the institutional management to allocate those resources within the institution.

There are several other important changes:
– a merger of very small institutes with fewer than two professors;
– not all faculty members will be civil servants; there is also the possibility of private contracts with the university;

– there will be more emphasis on teaching: a dean for teaching (*Studiendekan*) will be responsible for the co-ordination of all courses within a faculty.

The debate on the non-university sector

In the course of examining the Austrian higher education sector in 1975, the OECD examiners raised the question of how Austria would deal with the expansion of the post-secondary sector and the growing diversity of student needs. They made the expansion of the non-university post-secondary sector (NUS), which was then, and still is, quantitatively insignificant, a matter for discussion.

At that time Austria voiced the opinion that the study laws governing the university, despite their structural uniformity, permitted a diversity of offer.[2] An argument put forth against diversification of the post-secondary sector was that the system of Austrian technical/vocational schools was fulfilling the function of the NUS in other countries.

This objection had already defeated a reform proposal by an official of the Federal Ministry of Education and Arts in 1970, which would have created a NUS. It was not until 1988 and 1989 that the question of the non-university sector was taken up again. The following wording describes the position agreed on by experts of the social partners in 1989 in the framework of the report of the Advisory Council on Economic and Social Questions entitled *Qualifikation 2000*:

"The growing number of AHS graduates requires Austria, too, to offer this group of people new educational alternatives to university studies, alternatives which are rather underdeveloped in this country in contrast to neighbouring countries. (...) Furthermore, the structure of the post-secondary training sector in Austria should be checked in the light of international developments with respect to the question of whether the extension of the offer of short career-oriented studies and university courses and/or the creation of specific vocational academies ('technological, commercial, etc., academies') as an alternative to the training offered by universities could constitute reasonable measures towards better mutual attuning of the training system and the labour market."[3]

Originally there was a strong tendency to tackle the extension of non-university alternatives by widening existing offerings: colleges attached to technical schools, university courses, new forms of "dual" training programmes, and institutions of vocational adult education started to develop offerings within this new sector. However, the initial intention was not to set up a new coherent institutional framework. This attitude can be seen from an analysis of the political parties' programmes for education policy before the last parliamentary elections. But efforts were also made towards the creation of new institutions. One important factor was a recurring discussion of possibilities of relieving the universities and/or the drop-out problem. The body representing the interests of technical-school-trained engineers had been propounding a reform concept for some time proposing tertiary engineering training and a reform of technical industrial schools. This concept was also occasionally put forward in publications of employers' associations.

After a very short time – and initially without further work on concrete implementation – a general basic decision for the creation of such institutions (initially "Special Academies", later *Fachhochschulen*) was taken in the course of negotiations for the formation of a coalition government between the Social Democratic Party of Austria (SPÖ) and the Conservative Party (ÖVP), a decision which has also, by and large, found public assent.

The history of the discussion indicates that the EC Directive 89/48 on the recognition of diplomas was of decisive importance in taking this decision. The wording in the "Working Agreement" on the formation of a federal coalition government is as follows:

"The adaptation of the vocational system of education to the European standard (EC conformity of diplomas) requires the creation of Specialised Academies, which complement and relieve the university sector and should be established as institutions of training and continuing education for various vocational areas. Specialised Academies should essentially be open to graduates of upper secondary general and vocational schools as well as young skilled workers (after adequate qualification)."

A second factor is the development of a critical situation at universities, so that the desire for "relief" has become very strong. Finally, it seems that, with this project, a "positive" topic has re-entered education policy for the first time in years if not in decades. The shift of attention away from the many "unpleasant" problems of education policy towards this topic has also been very rapid.

Subsequent to this Agreement, discussion has developed in several waves: initial informal outlines for the design of the new institutions were developed in late 1990 and early 1991; the first presentations and publications occurred in mid-1991; revised and further elaborated statements were developed in the course of 1991; a common proposal of the Federal Ministry of Science and Research and of the Ministry of Education and Arts has been available, in the form of a ministerial draft, since spring 1992.

Chapter 3

ORGANISATION OF THE FACHHOCHSCHULEN

The accreditation model

The current debate on school and university organisation, which is characterised by increasing doubts as to whether the centralised and legally close-meshed education system is apt to meet the heterogeneous demands of students and society, has led the Federal Ministries of Science and Research and of Education and Arts to propose a *Fachhochschulen* sector based on an accreditation model. This model allows a large variety of institutions to offer courses, while at the same time ensuring unified standards of manageable complexity. Developments towards an expansion of the circle of suppliers of education programmes in the tertiary sector had already become visible by 1990 in an Amendment of the General University Studies Act (AHStG), which made it possible for non-university institutions to create university courses for continuing education after approval by the Federal Minister of Science and Research.

One of the basic principles of the accreditation model is thus to enable a large circle of educational institutions to offer *Fachhochschule* courses, so that the creation of *Fachhochschulen per se,* while not excluded, is not necessary for *Fachhochschule* courses to come into existence. Certainly schools and universities should be part of this circle, but also educational institutions run by the social partners and other interest groups, by provinces and communities, churches, private associations and private enterprises. If any of these institutions intends to offer a *Fachhochschule* course, the model provides that the interested party should submit an application to a *Fachhochschulrat,* which is to be established. This Council will examine the application for the quality of the intended syllabus, adequacy of access regulations, qualification of staff, existing infrastructure, cost estimates, and a plan for evaluation and further development of the curriculum. The *Fachhochschulrat* accreditation (for a limited period) observes performance and monitors evaluation. It does not make a decision about funding. It is up to the maintainer to ensure the necessary funding from his or her own funds, from subsidies by federal, provincial or local authorities or from other sources.

The *Fachhochschulrat* is intended as an autonomous board, which, although appointed by the Federal Ministers of Science and Research, and of Education and Arts, is not subject to instructions. It is to base its decisions on the criteria of scholarship and the correspondence between the curriculum and vocational requirements. Besides its above-mentioned tasks, this board would also have to ensure the further development of standards and the promotion and co-ordination of a nation-wide development. For this purpose it is further intended that continuous research be carried out for the evaluation of curricula and for the investigation of vocational areas, development work concerning innovations in teaching and further training measures for the teaching staff. The *Fachhochschulrat*'s activities are to be supported by a secretariat.

Under the model described, the development of every *Fachhochschule* course should be in the hands of a course team. This team should combine scholarly, practical vocational and pedagogical qualifications (at least two persons must have the academic qualification of an *Habilitation* and at least two must have vocational experience in the field). The course team would have authority for implementing the syllabus authorised by the *Fachhochschulrat*.

While the *Fachhochschulrat* would exercise formal control by providing or denying accreditation, it would exercise at least as much informal control. It would be especially important in the initial phase to set up and stimulate a process of discussion between the different course teams and the *Fachhochschulrat* as well as other experts from schools, universities and the various vocational areas concerned. The ruling principle should be that of delegation, with gradual extension of the powers of individual course teams. The aim of this process of discussion and its mutual control is the further development of standards for curricula and staff, where formal authority would lie with the *Fachhochschulrat*.

The difference between the accreditation model and the present university organisation

The relevant features of the Austrian education system, particularly of its higher education, are:
- nearly exclusive maintenance of educational facilities by federal authorities; this entails a centralised staff policy;
- high density of regulation in establishing the content of curricula; near-exclusive *ex ante* control;
- central administration of outside influence;
- large freedom of individual teachers and students;
- small powers of decentralised institutions compared with the power of the State and the freedom of individual teachers.

The accreditation model shows opposite tendencies to all these features.

Multiplicity of providers, decentralised staff and resource policy

The model proposes that a large number of private and public educational institutions may offer *Fachhochschule* courses. Not all of them have federal funding. But even where federal institutions run a course, these institutions would enjoy a higher degree of autonomy than is currently the case. In the initial phase there are two areas in which greater independence from federal authorities would exist. One would be staffing decisions: under the accreditation model the organiser proposes a course team, which must then be confirmed by the autonomous *Fachhochschulrat*. The second item concerns financial resources: it should be possible for all who intend to run a course to solicit funds from various sources. Of course, the federal government should not be released from its primary responsibility for tertiary education.

Variety of curricular initiatives and a combination of ex ante and ex post control

The present system is characterised by high density of regulation and the strong role of the State in establishing curricula and formulating their contents. By way of contrast the accreditation model provides for a variety of curricular initiatives by any possible *Fachhochschule* organisers. While these must be submitted to a central authority (the *Fachhochschulrat*) for accreditation, some of the features of this model are very different from the procedure currently used to set up curricula.

For one thing, the *Fachhochschulrat* is not directly subject to political influence, as it constitutes a board of experts not bound by instructions; it should, however, take the attitudes of political authorities into account in its decisions. For another, accreditations by the *Fachhochschulrat* are essentially for a limited period, tied to a mandate for evaluation. This permits greater risk and experimentation in the decision for accreditation. Thirdly, the *Fachhochschulrat* should not proceed by pre-defining a relatively narrow framework for possible curricula or voice the opinion that curricula must be quite similar. It should rather see itself as a body open to new proposals, which it will examine without prejudice. The above aspects would provide for a mix of *ex ante* and *ex post* quality control for the *Fachhochschule* courses.

Decentralisation of external influence

The strong role of the State in the Austrian education system is also reflected in the way it channels external influence. While the State's monopoly in dealing with external influence on the education system is also intended to protect university autonomy, it does reduce autonomy inasmuch as the State actually exerts its influence in matters of detail: understanding for the necessity and quality of autonomy of learning dwindles away among politicians and administrators. Moreover this "reduction of pressure" on universities implies that these institutions do not need to take a stand with respect to interests confronting them. This leads to a certain lack of responsibility towards society and thus simultaneously reduces the freedom of autonomous decisions concerning priorities. This attitude is abetted by the belief that a clear distinction between matters of education and matters of politics is possible.

The proposed model for the organisation of *Fachhochschule* courses involves greater external influence on curricula than is currently the case in university studies; at the same time, State influence should decrease. External influence is to be ensured by persons from the vocational area concerned who are active in the *Fachhochschulrat* as well as in the course teams. In addition, direct communication between the *Fachhoch-*

schulrat and representatives of the vocational areas is to take place. Finally, the occupational area and careers of graduates are a matter of investigation both for the *Fachhochschulrat* and the teaching staff of *Fachhochschule* courses. It is exactly this multiplicity of co-operation with external partners which reduces the role of the State as the sole source of external influence.

Individual freedom of teachers and learners

The Austrian education system is characterised by high power at the top, administered by the State, and by high power at the bottom of the organisation, represented at university level by tenured professors. The two are interconnected. The Austrian university professor reports to the State. He or she is appointed by the Federal President on the proposal of the Federal Minister for Science and Research. The influence of the university on his or her activities may be very low. Neither the head of the institute, the dean of the faculty, nor the rector of the university can give him or her direct instructions; at any rate there are hardly any sanctions besides the withdrawal of resources. As long as a professor teaches six to eight hours per week and conducts the relevant examinations, hardly anybody can call him or her to task. Although the same is not entirely true for assistants, they too enjoy considerable liberties, particularly those who have been appointed for life. Contractual instructors have to face more control as their appointment is only on a semester basis but they are also quite autonomous in their activities owing to the lack of supervision procedures and of persons interested in checks on instruction.

For students, the high degree of individual freedom is initially reflected in open access to university for all graduates of upper secondary schools, in the opportunity to make choices and to extend their study over a long period, as well as in the *de facto* form of examination which permits them to substitute the "collection of credits" for what should be comprehensive board examinations. The reverse side of the coin is well known: extremely long study times, high drop-out rates and a not uncommon lack of orientation.

What about the proposed *Fachhochschule* system? The model is based on the idea of co-operate autonomy rather than individual autonomy. This is first and foremost a matter concerning teachers. With regard to content, they would be more strictly bound by the curriculum. They could on the other hand take part in the actual definition of the curriculum, even if they are not members of the curriculum team.

Fachhochschule students should also be confronted with a system of stricter monitoring than current university students, starting with the admission procedures and continuing in a more streamlined curriculum and corresponding examination modes. The advantage for students is that this type of institution would ensure that studies be completed within a reasonable time-frame and that training meets vocational requirements. The coexistence of two systems with different degrees of individual commitment and obligation may be regarded as an advantage. After all, the possibility of opting for either system is given in both cases.

Strengthening the power of the "middle level"

At present comparatively high power at the top and bottom levels are matched by relatively little power at the "middle level", *i.e.* that of the individual educational institution (school, university, etc.) This intermediate level is to be strengthened in the proposed accreditation model, that is, the "middle level" is seen as the operating institution, represented in curricular matters by the course team. The means for strengthening this level in the accreditation model have already been set forth: the right to propose a curriculum, including the members of the course team, administration of allotted resources, elaboration of concrete syllabi, awarding of teaching contracts, detailing funding decisions. All of this constitutes a marked change from the current situation.

One prerequisite for exercising these powers, particularly as far as the course team is concerned, is the existence of a suitable identity for the social system in question. The current situation at the universities is characterised by many deficits.

Austrian universities have been described as a mixture of bureaucracy and anarchy. This is particularly evident in the combination of the high degree of State influence exercised by bureaucratic methods and the great individual freedom of university staff. On closer examination of the bureaucratic component of university life, a distinction can be made between a restricted bureaucracy (an administrative procedure determined in detail by legal regulations) and a formally democratic bureaucracy. The latter is largely taken to mean self-administration of the university by a large number of bodies, whose members are for the most part appointed by the three "estates", *i.e.* professors, medium-level teaching staff and students, in ratios of either 2:1:1 or 1:1:1. In the opinion of many university members, the formally democratic procedures are a forum for ritualised power struggles, infighting about resources and self-presentation while most consider them an unavoidable nuisance. The possibility of a debate concerning the merits of a common task is often forgotten in this context.

It is true that the situation is better at the lower levels of the hierarchy, where matters are more concrete. Thus, it is quite possible to hold discussions on the merits of a case in an institute conference or a study commission; but procedures remain similar to those used to manage a meeting involving an entire faculty. In the long term, individual and group interests and the logic of interaction resulting therefrom take pride of place: offering educational services is not sufficiently envisioned as a common task.

How could a *Fachhochschule* system improve the situation? First and foremost, no fixed structures and positions should be created that would put individual interests in conflict with group interests. Positively formulated: the success of the curriculum should benefit all persons engaged in the system. The most important measure in this respect is the undivided responsibility of the course team. Furthermore, the main distinction established within the team would be between teachers and students although a distinction should be made among teachers between team members and those hired afterwards. The latter would be heard in appropriate conferences but would not be included in the elaboration of the curriculum and thus bear limited responsibility. Membership in a course team should not be a permanent privilege – such as the analogous membership of a university professor in the top body of a faculty – neither should it be acquired by election within an interest group of which one is a member. Rather, membership in a course team should be acquired by demonstrating the ability to bring together a few colleagues, convince possible financiers, elaborate a curriculum and have it approved by the *Fachhochschulrat*.

On the role of education policy

In the initial discussion of the accreditation model, some critics noted, among other things, that the model would reduce the influence of both the lawmaker and government, and that a system might be created which would not be subject to democratic control. It is true and has been stated before that the model does envisage a reduction of legal and governmental activities in the education system in two main respects: the first concerning detailed regulations of contents, tests and organisation, and the other concerning staff decisions. Both changes are, however, compatible with tendencies which are under way in Austria, at least in such catchwords as "autonomy" and "rendering the attribution of posts more objective". On the other hand, the model does not preclude the influence of political bodies on the *Fachhochschule* system. For one thing, there is some influence on staff, viz. at the top level of the *Fachhochschulrat*: its members are to be appointed by the Ministers for Science and Research and for Education and Arts. But the major area of influence is via the allocation and control of public funds at the federal, provincial and community levels.

Besides these traditional channels for political influence – decisions concerning funding and staff – a further possibility should emerge, viz. on the basis of a high-quality discussion on educational policy. It might well be that throwing overboard the ballast of a continuously growing amount of detailed regulations – and of some dated ideological positions – might increase chances for more fundamental discussions.

Chapter 4

THE FINANCING OF THE FACHHOCHSCHULEN

A crucial issue in the present reform debate is the financial crisis in Austrian higher education. It is widely recognised that universities suffer from a lack of resources. There are two aspects to these financial constraints:

- The only source of income for universities is the federal budget. Since the university sector falls within federal responsibility, there are no financial contributions from the provinces. In the present NUS there is a more diverse pattern of finance, but only a small fraction of the money comes from sources other than the federal budget. On the other hand, there are no tuition fees in the university sector. This is a taboo issue which no political party wants to touch. Nearly all sides take it for granted that fees are an invincible barrier for poor students. There has not yet been a serious debate on contribution schemes, which would minimise undesirable social effects. However, some institutions in the NUS do charge tuition fees.
- Due to a highly inflexible way of financing the education system, and the universities in particular, federal authorities have lost budgetary manœuvrability to a large extent. There is a direct connection between the organisational law and the financial obligations for the Federal State. Thus, the major part of the federal budget is not negotiable and only a small fraction of the money is available for new developments. Due to the organisational inflexibility and the fact that nearly all teachers are tenured, it is very difficult to abandon or even modify an activity once it has been established.

Before passing any law and, in particular, before establishing a new education sector, lawmakers are faced with the question of the strains these measures may produce on the budget. Future financial obligations are especially important in a time of budgetary tension. In the late 1960s and early 1970s there was a short period when a reform-oriented policy was matched by rising budgets. In the 1980s the financial constraints of the federal budget became a strong impediment for educational reforms. The inflexibility of the organisational and financial mechanisms explain why authorities are more and more reluctant to establish new areas. The authorities could easily lose control over costs.

In the area of *Fachhochschulen,* increased organisational flexibility is to be accompanied by increased flexibility in financial decision-making. One basic prerequisite for attaining this objective is the uncoupling of organisational regulations from decisions concerning the level of financial engagement of federal authorities. While the former imposes no financial obligation on federal authorities – except for the expenditures of the accreditation body – a plan regarding the financial involvement of the federal government determines how many student places are to be funded by federal authorities.

Until now no consensus was reached concerning the nature of the financial engagement. One idea favoured by some experts suggests that the Federal State should "purchase" study places from the institutions. Such a concept raises many technical questions which, strictly speaking, are not yet resolved. However, some preliminary studies have been commissioned to estimate the average cost per student, taking account of different cost elements and different didactic methods. These costs may be subdivided according to the following categories:

- Annual running costs comprising staff costs for both scientific and non-scientific staff, building operation expenses (cleaning, maintenance and repair), library expenses, running investment costs and other operating costs (telephone, materials for use and consumption, etc.).
- Construction costs comprising the net construction and/or reconstruction costs for existing buildings. This does not include planning costs, which amount to approximately 10 per cent of (net) construction costs.
- Initial investment costs essentially comprising expenses for electronic data processing, audio-visual equipment, furniture, laboratory equipment and initial library equipment.

Different didactic models are represented by a "school model" and a "university model":

- The school model refers to a comparatively school-like form of organisation. Basically, it is characterised by compact training in small groups not exceeding thirty people. An immanent feature of "compact training" is the intensive attention given to the training potential both in terms of material and in terms of time and staff.

  This requires that training be accompanied, among other things, by written material, thus minimising the autonomous study of literature and reducing the requirement for library resources. The teaching staff is characterised by ensuring application and demand-oriented training rather than engaging in research tasks.
- The university model is based on a somewhat looser organisation of instruction. Students have the opportunity to study individually through implemented degrees of freedom both materially and in terms of time and staff. Instruction takes place in groups of various sizes. The model uses a maximum group size of 100 persons for lectures, 30 persons for exercises and practical work and 15 persons for seminar-type classes. In addition, ten library hours per week are set down for each training place. In addition to their training function, the teaching staff is engaged in application- and demand-oriented research.

Costs per student

in Austrian Schillings

Cost elements	School model		University model	
	Upper limit	Lower limit	Upper limit	Lower limit
Annual costs	93 000	72 000 000	88 000	63 000
Construction costs	158 000	137 000	139 000	103 000
Initial investment costs	38 000	20 000	55 000	22 000
Minimum student capacity	1 000		900	

The difference in construction costs per student between the school model and the university model is mainly caused by the different group sizes to be provided for under the respective concepts. In the school model, training basically takes place in small groups, with the consequence that considerably more instruction area must be supplied than in the university model.

The slightly higher initial investment costs in the university model are a result of the binding of resources by teaching staff, which – because of their research activities and the comparatively low teaching load – is higher than in the school model. In essence this covers furniture costs and the technical support of teaching and research operations.

Postscript

In March 1993 the coalition government introduced the *Fachhochschule* bill and Parliament passed it in mid-May. The law (*Bundesgesetz über Fachhochschulstudien-gänge,* FHSTG) corresponds with the draft which has been described above. The next steps will be the establishment of the *Fachhochschulrat.* First activities in designing *Fachhochschule* courses are under way. However, vital issues like possible patterns of mixed funding and the financial involvement of the federal government have still to be tackled.

The proposal on a reform of the organisation of universities has been revised several times. At the beginning of June 1993 the coalition government passed the final draft which will be presented to Parliament. With this draft, some changes stated in former proposals and described above have been cancelled. The most important changes concern the *Universitäten-Kuratorium* and the appointment and responsibilities of the rector: the *Universitäten-Kuratorium* is to be an advisory body; the rector is to be elected by the university assembly and his responsibilities are to be restricted as compared to the former drafts.

Notes

1. Nursery schools are not legally part of the education system.
2. *Reviews of National Policies for Education: Austria – Higher Education and Research,* OECD, Paris, 1976.
3. *Qualifikation 2000,* Beirat für Wirtschafts und Sozialfragen, Wien, 1989, pp. 24-26.

Annex 1. SCHEME OF THE AUSTRIAN EDUCATIONAL SYSTEM

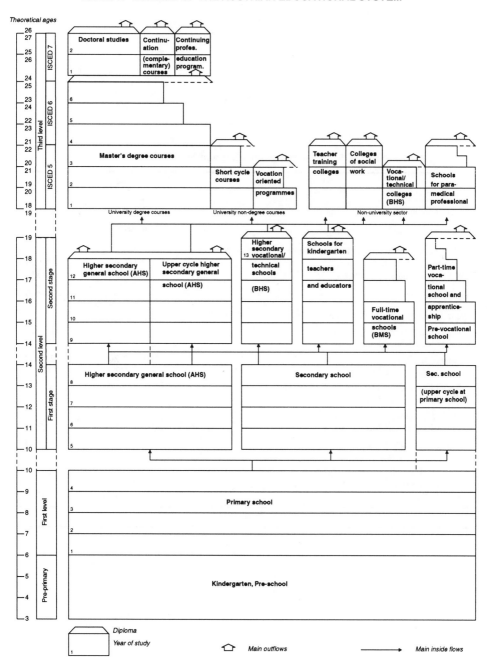

Annex 2

Table A.1. **Resident population and labour force, 1990**

	Total	Female
Resident population, total	7 718 300	4 024 600
Resident population over 15 years	6 288 900	3 313 500
Resident population with a university degree or a certificate of post-secondary institution	314 400	125 900
(% of total resident population)	(5.0)	(3.8)
Labour force, total	3 523 000	1 439 400
Labour force, by level of education		
– Compulsory school	1 004 000	512 400
(% of total labour force)	(28.5)	(35.6)
– Apprenticeship	1 483 200	424 600
(% of total labour force)	(42.1)	(29.5)
– Secondary schools of vocational education	236 000	384 400
(% of total labour force)	(10.9)	(16.4)
– Higher secondary general school	176 100	83 500
(% of total labour force)	(5.0)	(5.8)
– Higher secondary vocational school	225 500	87 800
(% of total labour force)	(6.4)	(6.1)
– Universities, colleges of art and music, non-university post-secondary	250 100	95 000
(% of total labour force)	(7.1)	(6.6)

Source: Austrian Statistical Office, Microcensus 1990, Vienna, 1991.

Table A.2. **Labour force and qualifications, 1990**

	Total	Female
Self-employed: agriculture and forestry [1]	235 700	120 800
Self-employed: commerce, trade, industry [1]	208 300	78 000
Professional workers [1]	51 200	15 100
White-collar employees, total	1 066 600	585 400
thereof:		
– highly-qualified or managerial	128 800	19 000
– professionally qualified	174 500	57 100
– other white-collar employees	763 300	509 300
Civil servants,	627 000	259 700
thereof:		
– highly-qualified or managerial	41 500	9 000
– professionally qualified	185 300	91 200
– other civil servants	400 200	159 500
Blue-collar workers,	1 347 100	389 000
thereof:		
– foremen, craftsmen	562 40	68 700
– other blue-collar workers	784 700	320 300

1. Including family workers.
Source: Austrian Statistical Office, Microcensus 1990, Vienna, 1991.

Table A.3. **Number of pupils/students by type of institution,**
Academic year 1990/91

Type of school	Pupils/students	
	Total	Female
Elementary school	371 971	181 269
Secondary school [1]	258 426	121 220
Shools for handicapped children	18 322	7 175
Secondary general schools (AHS) – low cycle	92 878	46 509
Compulsory schools, total	741 597	356 173
Part-time vocational schools (apprenticeship)	152 804	53 625
Secondary general schools (AHS) – upper cycle [2]	62 506	34 101
Secondary technical/vocational schools (BMS) [2]	47 483	29 833
Higher secondary technical/vocational schools (BHS) [2]	86 771	41 767
Schools for educators and kindergarten-teachers [2]	4 949	4 837
Upper secondary schools, total	201 709	110 538
Non-university post-secondary institutions	13 844	9 768
Universities	170 718	75 499
Colleges of art and music	4 683	2 205

1. Including 9th grade (*Polytechnischer Lehrgang*).
2. Excluding special types of schools for adults.

Table A.4. **New entrants, students and graduates of post-secondary institutions in Austria**
Academic year 1990/91

	New entrants		Students		Graduates [1]	
	Total	Female	Total	Female	Total	Female
Universities	19 688	9 593	170 718	75 499	10 239	4 292
Colleges of art and music	525	259	4 683	2 205	403	192
Teacher training college	1 929	1 600	4 958	4 135	1 524	1 281
Teacher training college (for vocational schools)	346	160	836	434	306	141
Teacher training colleges (for religious instruction)	142	119	487	410	121	101
Colleges of social work	366	281	933	711	215	166
Technical colleges [2]	3 246	1 595	5 012	2 624	2 141	1 065
Schools for paramedical professions	737	653	1 618	1 454	583	535
Total	26 979	14 260	189 245	87 472	15 532	7 773

1. First and second degrees at universities and colleges of art and music; other institutions: final year students.
2. Courses for higher school graduates at higher secondary technical/vocational schools.

Table A.5. **Educational attainment of young people in Austria, 1990**
Percentages

	Total	Female
Percentage of the 16-year-old population in education 1990 [1]	96.3	92.1
– Vocational schools	12.9	17.7
– Higher secondary technical/vocational schools [2]	20.4	19.2
– Higher secondary general schools	16.1	18.8
– Apprenticeship	46.9	36.4
Percentage of high school graduates of age group, [3] 1990	30.7	32.8
– Graduates of higher secondary general schools	12.8	14.4
– Graduates of higher secondary technical/vocational schools [2]	14.9	15.9
Percentage of new entrants to non-university institutions of age group, 1990 [3, 4]	5.7	7.8
Percentage of new entrants to universities and colleges of art and music of age group, 1990 [5]	18.5	18.4
Percentage of students at universities and colleges of art and music of age group, 1990 [6]	18.8	16.9

1. 16-year-old resident population, average 1990. Breakdown by sex is estimated. *Source*: Austrian Statistical Office.
2. Including schools for kindergarten teachers and educators.
3. Average of 18- to 19-year-old resident population 1990.
4. Excluding teacher training colleges for vocational education.
5. Average of 18- to 21-year-old resident population 1990.
6. Percentage of the total number of students of the 18- to 25-year-old resident population. The percentage of the 18- to 25-year-old student population in the 18- to 25-year-old resident population is 11.4 and 10.8 (female).

Table A.6. **Fields of study of new entrants to universities by type of their secondary education**
Winter term 1990/91

Type of secondary education/school	Law		Social science, economics		Medecine		Theology, humanities		Engineering, technology[1]		Agriculture, forestry		Veterinary		Total	
	Number	%	Number	%	Number	%	Number	%	Number	%	Number	%	Number	%	Number	%
HSS* of general education																
5th to 12th grade type	1 575	16	1 683	17	750	7	3 659	36	1 938	19	414	4	127	1	10 146	100
9th to 12th grade type	459	15	418	14	201	7	1 388	46	391	13	80	3	53	2	2 990	100
Special types	45	20	27	12	12	5	111	49	26	12	4	2	1		226	100
HSS of general education, total	2 079	16	2 128	16	963	7	5 158	39	2 355	18	498	4	181	1	13 362	100
HSS of vocational education																
Commercial	290	10	1 581	56	29	1	649	23	224	8	37	1	9		2 819	100
Engineering, tech., arts	147	4	852	25	17	1	496	15	1 751	51	149	4	2		3 414	100
Home economics	104	9	333	29	20	2	593	52	61	5	16	1	8	1	1 135	100
Agriculture and forestry	12	6	49	24	5	2	45	22	20	9	59	29	13	6	203	100
HSS for educators and kindergarten teachers	18	7	10	4	4	2	201	83	9	4	1				243	100
HSS of vocational education, total	571	7	2 825	36	75	1	1 984	25	2 065	26	262	3	32		7 814	100
External examinations	18	23	16	21	4	5	34	44	5	6					77	100
Access exams to universities for non-traditional students	55	45	21	17	13	11	27	22	2	2	1	1	2	2	121	100
Total	2 764	13	5 044	23	1 107	5	7 393	34	4 489	21	764	4	221	1	21 782	100

* Higher Secondary Schools.
1. Including mining.
Source: Austrian Statistical Office.

Table A.7. **Degree courses enrolled in by Austrian new entrants, students and graduates, by group of subjects**[1]
Winter term 1990/91

Group of subjects	New entrants	Students	First degrees
Theology	215	3 201	185
Doctoral courses		294	
Law	2 690	21 211	1 057
Doctorat courses		1 688	
Social sciences, economics	4 899	41 196	1 712
Doctoral courses		2 390	
Medicine	1 078	13 382	1 383
Philosophy/humanities	2 020	21 128	623
History/art	923	11 088	446
Philology/Cultural studies	1 506	12 066	512
Translation, interpretation	323	3 674	120
Natural sciences	1 814	15 205	595
Pharmacy	254	2 472	168
Sports, physical training	112	2 712	161
Humanities and natural sciences, total	6 952	68 345	2 634
Doctoral courses, humanities and natural sciences		3 797	
Building engineering, architecture, landscape architecture	1 171	8 717	302
Mechanical engineering	621	5 389	242
Electrical engineering	433	4 443	263
Science/Technology	1 844	11 325	404
Technical short cycle courses	110	1 386	40
Technology, engineering, total	4 179	31 260	1 251
Technology, engineering: doctoral courses		1 934	
Mining, petroleum, metallurgy engineering	234	1 910	79
Mining, petroleum, metallurgy engineering: doctoral courses		49	
Agriculture/forestry	736	5 542	305
Agriculture/forestry: doctoral courses		288	
Veterinary medicine	217	2 280	114
Veterinary medicine: doctoral courses		174	
Studium irregulare (individually designed curricula)		611	
Continuing training (post-graduate)		922	
Total	21 200	200 544	8 748
of which: doctoral courses		10 614	

1. Including text courses (*Studienversuche*).

Table A.8. **Expenditure for education**

in billion AS

	1990	1991	1992
GNP nominal	1 789.4	1 905.1	2 038.1
Federal budget	564.7	600.3	635.9
Federal expenditure for education	48.5	52.6	54.3[1]
Federal expenditure for universities and colleges of art and music	18.9	22.2	24.1[2]
Public expenditure for education, total[3]	97 309.0		

1. *Of which:* AS 20.4 billion personnel expenditure, as 33.9 billion capital expenditure.
2. *Of which:* AS 9.4 billion personnel expenditure, AS 11 billion capital expenditure, AS 1.3 billion building expenditure and AS 2.4 billion promotion of research.
3. Including expenditure of provinces and communities, data for 1991 and 1992 not yet available.

Part Two

THE EXAMINERS' REPORT

Chapter 1

INTRODUCTION

"(...) the kind of experiment from which we can learn most is the alteration of one social institution at a time. For only in this way can we learn how to fit institutions into the framework of other institutions, and how to adjust them so that they work according to our intentions. And only in this way can we make mistakes and learn from our mistakes, without risking repercussions of a gravity that must endanger the will to future reforms (...)".

Karl Popper
(*The Open Society and its Enemies,*
Vol. 1, Routledge, 1962, p. 163)

Austria is a small country – it has a population of less than 8 million – yet it is often described as the crossroads of Europe. Recent geo-political developments have heightened the relevance of this metaphor. The changes in Eastern Europe mean that Austria has an increasingly important function as a nexus of trade and political exchange. At the same time, Austria is seeking to strengthen its economic and political connections within Western Europe: it entered the European Economic Space in 1993, after which it has become a member of the European Union.

These changes present Austria with both opportunities and challenges. They open wider markets for Austrian goods, but also open the Austrian economy to increased competition. In particular, the Austrian education system is affected by the EU directives on the harmonization of qualifications. Whilst these are not the only factors affecting the development of the higher education system in Austria, they have had a significant role in catalysing the process of reform we are concerned with.

Austria faces problems of a budget deficit and the government is committed to reducing this as a proportion of GDP (OECD, 1991). There is a recognition of the need for more efficient use of public resources. Subsidies and regulation are considered excessive and the government's programme aims to strengthen competitiveness through reform of competition and pricing laws. More financial responsibility is to be given to the provinces to achieve a better match between spending decisions and financial responsibility.

Higher education in Austria

In many ways, Austria is a well educated society: only about 2 per cent of students leave the education system after the end of compulsory schooling. The number of students completing higher secondary education (to age 18 or 19) has more than doubled in the last 20 years, currently representing some 31 per cent of their age group. Nearly 200 000 students are enrolled in Austrian universities of whom over 176 000 are Austrian citizens. Students aged 18-25 represent about 12 per cent of their age group.

But figures, as always, can be deceptive. The secondary education system in Austria is divided into three main parts. At age 14, students who intend to go on to full-time education enter either four years of general education (AHS) or vocational education, where they take four-year courses (BMS) or five-year courses (BHS). All students completing the four-year AHS and the five-year BHS gain the *Matura* qualification and are entitled to enter university. Nearly half of all 14-year-olds enter the "dual" system of apprenticeship. Most of them receive one year of pre-vocational education, after which they become employed and receive only part-time, though compulsory, education. Most do not continue on to any higher level of education.

Like some other OECD countries, the Austrian university system is plagued with the problem of high drop-out rates and long duration of study: only 9 000 students graduated from Austrian universities in 1992. Since there were almost as many academic staff in these universities, the average Austrian academic could be said to "produce" only one graduate per year.

The quality of students from Austrian education institutions appears to be widely recognised. Apprentices are generally valued by employers. Students completing the BHS are acknowledged as highly competent in their specialised fields and are employed in both Austria and abroad in jobs where they compete with graduates from German *Fachhochschule*. Graduates from Austrian universities are acknowledged as having a high-level academic education and because their numbers are relatively small, are often felt by employers to be in short supply. However, the training provided in both streams is often criticised for its narrowness.

Austria, unlike other OECD countries, has a relatively small non-university higher education sector. Just under 14 000 students were enrolled in non-university post-secondary institutions (with another 4 700 in colleges of music and art) in 1990/91. Proposals to create a more diversified post-secondary system were developed in the 1970s, but defeated on the grounds that the Austrian system of secondary technical and vocational schools fulfilled the function of a non-university sector in other countries.

Reforming higher education

As in its geo-politics, Austria is also at a crossroads in terms of education policy. The coalition government's "work-programme" places considerable emphasis on reforming the education system. Central features of this programme are a move away from the traditional Austrian political culture of centralisation and detailed regulation.

In higher education, this reform programme currently involves two major policy proposals. The more advanced is the proposal to create a new non-university sector of higher education in *Fachhochschulen*. A draft law to establish an accrediting body to supervise the academic development of this sector was circulated for "expert comment" in September 1992 and was presented to Parliament in early 1993.

Austria's intention to join the EU triggered renewed discussion on the development of a non-university sector. In June 1988, the EU Council of Ministers for Economic Affairs reached agreement on the mutual recognition of higher education diplomas in the twelve member States. The Directive which issued from this requires three years of post-secondary education for recognition of qualifications at this level. The graduates from Austria's upper vocational secondary schools appeared not to meet this requirement.

The second proposal is to reform the management of universities; a consultation document on this (the "orange paper") was circulated for comment in 1992. A draft law was circulated for comment early in 1993, after the examiners' visit (and hence is not considered in this report).

These proposals have generated considerable debate in Austria, the nature of which is important. There appears to be reasonable agreement on the need for reform but less about the method by which reform should be carried out. We detected, for example, widespread acknowledgement of the need for a *Fachhochschule* sector of some sort, yet divergence of opinion on the particular proposals in the draft law. Similarly, whilst there was agreement on the need for greater managerial autonomy for universities, there were strong feelings on the detail of the proposals; the debate here was also complicated by financial factors, with fears, as in other OECD countries, that autonomy merely delegated decisions about financial constraint.

The debate has highlighted the fact that reform of the higher education system raises wider issues of which the most crucial are decentralisation and deregulation. In this sense, the reforms place Austria at another important crossroads, about the way in which it will be governed and administered.

Chapter 2

DEREGULATION AND DECENTRALISATION

The Austrian tradition

The Austrian education system is characterised by a tradition of an explicit legal basis for all government initiatives. There is a great diversity of educational institutions, mostly public, which results of a rather pragmatic response to educational needs, as well as a high degree of regulation by detailed laws.

In these circumstances, the realisation of any change in the education system is difficult. Modifications mostly require new legislation, which in the case of school (though not university) education, has to be approved by a majority of two-thirds in Parliament. For a foreign observer the latter constitutional prescription is surprising because the education system needs to adapt to rapidly changing demands. Such a majority forces the government to obtain a very broad consensus on its proposals and, as a result, it has to advance step by step. The well developed system of consultation of the social partners before any important decision is taken by the federal authorities also helps to ensure that nothing can happen unless a general consensus exists. Perhaps this attitude is also influenced by a remnant of the historical popular belief in imperial solicitude for the welfare of the people.

However, there is a need for rather far-reaching innovations to be introduced. Because of its entry into the European Economic Space (EES) and into the European Union, a large number of laws (about 110) have to be adapted in order to conform with existing EU regulations. By comparison, Switzerland, with a less detailed legal basis, has only slightly more than half as many laws to change. This raises the question of whether a change from the present system of very detailed legislation would not reduce this difficulty. Such a move would reflect the currently popular calls for deregulation.

The Maastricht Treaty has provoked a vivid discussion about the dangers of excessive central bureaucracy. It would thus be somewhat contradictory if national administrations continued unchallenged centralised reigns. In the case of education, the EU authorities accept the autonomy of the different national education systems. When preparing for participation in the EES and the Common Market, the Austrian authorities therefore face the question of how the education system should be modified to achieve consistency with EU principles even though some EU countries still use a highly centralised education administration.

The need for autonomy

Individual educational institutions, including the universities, have very limited responsibility for their own budgets and management. The public education system is centrally directed and largely financed by the two education ministries – the Ministry for Education and Arts (BMUK) (primary and secondary education) and the Ministry for Science and Research (BMWF) (universities and colleges of art and music).

The convention of the coalition parties (the *Arbeitsübereinkommen der Regierung*) proposes to increase the autonomy of individual educational institutions throughout the system. In particular, universities are to be made increasingly responsible for their performance. The government considers this an essential part of reforms aimed at increasing the efficiency of the university system. To realise this fundamental change, they want to create a management structure for each university with a reasonable degree of autonomy in matters of budget, personnel and organisation.

Although the lack of institutional autonomy is increasingly criticised, the examiners noted that educational institution staff seemed reluctant to take on new responsibilities. Many people we spoke to seemed to place more trust in the ministries rather than in their own capacity to govern.

The introduction of more autonomy for educational institutions encounters additional opposition due to the financial difficulties of the Austrian government. This has created the suspicion that the ministries want to give up some of their power in order to avoid responsibility for cuts in the budgets of educational institutions. Some heads of institutions are afraid that they may have "to administer the want" if given more autonomy now. They do not share the conviction that the authorities closest to the institution are in the best position to distribute the available funds. This tenet, which is the basis of any concept of decentralisation, may not be so important when abundant financial means are available. However, if public funds are scarce, then their flexible deployment may ensure that the most urgent needs are still met and who, other than education management at the local and institutional levels, is sufficiently informed to accomplish this?

A comparison of statistics on the Austrian education system with other European countries provides further arguments for devolution. For instance, the individual compulsory school teacher has to look after only half of the number of pupils (about 10 on the average) of his colleague in Germany or France. If the local authorities had to pay these teachers instead of the federal government, this situation might be different.

Decentralisation is only sensible if management is sufficiently competent, which requires an appropriate training of those who will be in charge. The best solution would probably be to make this training available within the framework of continuing education to prepare teachers showing both interest and capabilities for such tasks.

New sources of finance

Many OECD countries face the problem of financing higher education, and increasingly accept the idea that funds must come from a diversity of sources. The concept of decentralisation may be of particular interest now because of the deficits in the budget of the Austrian government.

Educational institutions at all levels are almost totally financed by the federal government. In some quarters, such as trade unions or student organisations, there is a strong preference for maintaining this situation. This means that any new institution has to be financed completely or largely by the federal authorities. Under these circumstances substantial reforms can be difficult. The introduction of *Fachhochschulen,* for example, cannot be easily realised; the Ministry of Finance made clear that additional funds for creating such new institutions cannot be found unless corresponding cuts in the allotments for existing educational institutions are possible. With rare exceptions the examiners did not find a readiness for such reductions. But the few concrete proposals for a *Fachhochschule* show that it is possible to find other funding sources since they include a substantial element of regional resources.

Some of the funds will necessarily have to come from sources other than the federal budget if the financial barrier to innovation is to be overcome. The *Bundesländer* or communal authorities are an obvious possible source; if they contributed to such new institutions this would also help to avoid an excessive covetousness which is to be expected if the federal government entirely foots the bill for the new *Fachhochschulen.*

Private funding in higher education also has to be considered and there is a readiness in the private sector to contribute to the cost of higher education. Granted, employers will not take on long-term recurrent funding commitments, on grounds of the unpredictability of their profits and on the principle that they should not fund "basic" education. However, large employers already contribute to university and to vocational education. They indicated a particular willingness in relation to *Fachhochschulen,* offering capital funding, and contributions "in kind", such as giving equipment, letting some of their qualified staff teach, by supporting employees who want to study at such places and by offering paid contracts for specific services.

A systematic search for new income cannot leave aside the question of contributions from the prime beneficiaries of higher education, in other words the question of student fees. This discussion is almost taboo in Austria, above all in political circles. However, to pay fees for education is not entirely unknown since universities charge for some non-degree courses offering professional training and some vocational secondary schools request a fee for curricula in commercial trades. Fees are known in practically all OECD Member countries at the post-secondary level, but vary widely between nominal amounts to considerable charges which largely cover the costs. It is also argued that fees (even moderate ones) may exert pressure on the students to finish their education within a reasonable time.

Some advocates of applying a market philosophy to the education system propose that the State should finance students (through a voucher system), rather than institutions, so students would be free to attend the establishment of their choice. Such a proposal has clear shortcomings. In particular it eliminates the possibility of government influencing the development of curricula important for the country or to bring about reforms required by a changed environment. A mixed system, with fees paid by students and direct public support of the education system is more or less universal in OECD countries, and reflects the fact that the educational institutions on the post-secondary level fulfil important research and service functions for the public. Their future should not only depend on their popularity among students.

There are obvious objections to the principle of student fees, mostly on social grounds. A well-developed system of public scholarships, which would take fees into account, should be made available in order to avoid financial hardship preventing students from going on to higher education. A thorough revision of existing public subsidies for students, in order to eliminate a too widespread distribution, may even help to find some of the money required without greatly increasing the burden on the governmental budget. In Austria students are already supported by the government in a number of ways, even to the point where some maintain their status although they no longer have the intention of graduating. The range of the fees and system of scholarships could be adjusted so that such behaviour would no longer be attractive.

Chapter 3

HIGHER EDUCATION AND THE ECONOMY

The Background Report (Part One) does not give an indulgent picture of the Austrian economy. The picture may be unduly pessimistic, yet it highlights structural imbalances, such as the high share in production and exports taken by industries with a low manufacturing value added, the lag in the capital goods and high-tech sectors, low labour productivity, rigidities of all kinds in an economy which has long been closely regulated and whose particularly inefficient nationalised sector has been in a critical situation for several years.

Austria of course does not belong to the leading group of highly developed countries in terms of per capita Gross Domestic Product (GDP). Nevertheless, Austria ranked 9th out 24 in 1991 according to such a criterion. Its per capita GDP was similar to that of Belgium in Table 1. Nonetheless, as noted by the OECD (1991), its economic growth is buoyant, its balance of payments is in equilibrium, and unemployment, although rising, is still lower than in many Western European countries.

Austria has a higher percentage of manufacturing industry than most OECD countries, though like most others, this percentage is declining. Unusually, there is higher growth in this sector than in the economy as a whole and there is a marked shift to capital goods industries. In 1988, 37 per cent of the workforce was employed in this sector. Apart from this, only the wholesale and retail sector on the one hand and the hotel and restaurant sector on the other (24 per cent) were the only sectors to employ significantly more than 10 per cent of the total workforce. Austrian wage costs have, on the whole, risen less than in competitor countries. Table 1 gives some comparative data on some of these and other topics for Austria and a sample of similar OECD countries.

The role of small firms in the Austrian economy is important but must not be overestimated. In 1989, over 40 per cent of Austrian enterprises had four or fewer employees while 98 per cent had fewer than 500. However, the 2 per cent of firms with more than 500 employees had 38 per cent of the workforce while the corresponding figure for firms with 50 to 499 employees was nearly 50 per cent.

The Background Report expresses concern about medium-term economic prospects; following agreement on the European Economic Space and membership of European Union, Austria may feel the pressure on employment from an inflow of immigrants that could be difficult to control. There is concern about the production system's development

Table 1. A selection of comparative data in some OECD countries, 1991

	EFTA Countries					EU countries	
	Austria	Finland	Norway	Sweden	Switzerland	Belgium	Denmark
1. Population (1991) (thousands)	7.823	4.986	4.262	8.588	6.860	9.840	5.154
2. Employment (1990)							
% agriculture	7.9	8.4	6.5	3.3	5.6	2.7	5.6
% industry	36.8	31.0	24.8	29.1	35.0	28.3	27.5
% services	55.3	60.6	68.8	67.5	59.5	69.0	66.9
3. Gross Domestic Product (GDP) per capita (1991) (US$) at 1985 price levels and converted using PPPS	14 133	12 904	13 561	13 797	17 436	14 138	14 074
4. Exports of goods (1990) as % of GDP	26.0	19.4	32.1	25.2	28.4	61.5	27.1
5. Imports of goods (1990) as % of GDP	31.1	19.6	25.7	24.0	31.0	62.5	24.5
6. Gross expenditure on R&D (1989) as % of GDP	1.37	1.80	1.86	2.85	2.86	1.69	1.54
7. Public expenditures on education (1991) as % of GDP	5.4	6.1	6.8	6.5	5.4	5.4	6.1
8. Percentage of the population 25 to 64 years of age having completed a certain highest level of of education (1991)							
Upper sec. (ISCED 3)	61	42	54	44	60	24	43
Non-univ. (ISCED 5)	–	8	12	11	13	10	6
Univ. (ISCED 6/7)	7	10	12	12	7	10	13

Sources: Lines 2, 4, 5: OECD Basic Statistics: International Comparisons.
Lines 1, 3, 8: *Education at a Glance. OECD Indicators*, OECD, Paris, 1993.
Lines 6, 7: OECD: EAS Database.

and innovation potential and the relative weakness of R&D in both the public and private sectors, which is resulting in a negative balance of trade in patents. Even with modest ambitions for the economy and for the diffusion of innovation, specialisation and flexibility in industry or for the development of tourism and services, rather than the promotion of strategic industries and spectacular scientific breakthroughs, R&D must be strengthened in terms of staff and funding.

According to the OECD (1988), R&D expenditure in manufacturing as a whole has risen steadily, from 3.7 per cent of production value in 1981 to 5.41 per cent in 1988. Major firms seem to account for the bulk of this increase, even if some of them belong to multinational groups that conduct most of their research in other countries. Whilst those major firms we visited seemed efficient, the sectors which have been protected and the vast majority of small firms are probably not sufficiently innovation-minded, which is perhaps one reason why the productivity increase is so low. The authors of the Background Report point out that R&D expenditures as a proportion of GNP did not exceed 1.4 per cent at the end of the 1980s, or half the figure for the most advanced countries. As indicated in Table 1, line 6, in 1989 Austria ranked last in the group of countries chosen for comparative purposes. The OECD (1988) was of the view that this needed to increase faster than GDP. Since the 1980s, the government has made the encouragement of the conversion of scientific knowledge into product and process innovation a priority in research programmes. In this respect, despite unquestionable advantages, entry into the European Union might prove painful.

Education in the economy

Table 1 (line 7) shows that the percentage of GDP spent on education in Austria compares well with that of Belgium and Switzerland but is clearly lower that that of the four Nordic countries. Spending on higher education appears to be at least comparable with that of similar countries (Table 2), though the spending per student (column 2) seems lower than that of the other countries.

Although the number of graduates emerging from Austrian higher education is relatively low, the number of students enrolled in the upper secondary sector is relatively high, as indicated in Table 3. Tables 4, 5 and 6 illustrate Austria's low take-up rate in both university and non-university higher education. The tables underline that Austria is lagging behind the other countries in the development of the non-university tertiary education. Austria's apparently advanced position in university enrolments in Table 5 in fact largely reflects the extended length of study in the universities, and needs to be compared with the number of graduates (Table 6).

Austria has a relatively low proportion of graduates in science and engineering compared to similar countries, except Norway (Table 7) and a low proportion of women graduating in engineering (except Switzerland) (Table 8).

Table 2. **National effort in higher education, 1991**

(indicators P3, P6 and P7)

	Share of expenditure on tertiary education	Expenditure per student	
		In equivalent US$*	Relative to per-capita GDP
Austria	**22.7** (PUB)	**6 441**	**37.3**
Other EFTA			
Finland	23.7	7 218**	43.0**
Norway	19.8 (PUB)	8 405	50.0
Sweden	18.3	8 561	52.6
Switzerland	22.5 (PUB)	14 682	67.6
EU countries			
Belgium	19.0 (PUB)	6 235	35.8
Denmark	21.4	7 685	43.7

*   Converted, using purchasing power parities (PPPs).
**   Expenditure per student from public and privates sources.
(PUB)   means that the percentages refer to shares of public expenditure only.
Source: Education at a Glance – OECD indicators, OECD, Paris, 1993.

Table 3. **Upper secondary school enrolments (full-time equivalents) per 100 persons of corresponding age, public and private schools, 1991**

(indicator P11)

	General education	Vocational/technical education and apprenticeship	Total
Austria	**28.7**	**100.5**	**120.0**
Other EFTA			
Finland	56.9	101.9	152.3
Norway	48.0	73.8	121.8
Sweden	22.4	74.1	98.2
Switzerland	21.6	87.7	107.4
EU countries			
Belgium	46.6	56.6	99.1
Denmark	33.7	57.6	90.9

Source: Education at a Glance, op. cit.

Table 4. **Number of first entrants into full-time public and private tertiary education per 100 persons in the theoretical starting age, by gender, 1991**

(indicator P15)

	Non-university education			University education			Total		
	M + W	M	W	M+W	M	W	M + W	M	W
Austria	**4.5**	**3.5**	**5.6**	**23.2**	**23.5**	**22.9**	**27.7**	**27.0**	**28.5**
Other EFTA									
Finland	29.0	19.6	38.6	33.2	34.2	32.2	62.2	53.8	70.8
Norway	17.5	15.1	20.1	19.2	16.6	22.0	36.7	31.7	42.0
Sweden	33.7	29.5	38.2	13.4	13.2	13.6	47.1	42.7	51.9
Switzerland	12.8	15.1	10.4	14.1	15.6	12.5	26.9	30.7	22.9
EU countries									
Belgium	22.5	17.5	27.9	25.8	27.7	23.9	48.4	45.2	51.7
Denmark	13.6	12.9	14.4	24.4	20.0	29.2	38.0	32.9	43.5
Mean for all OECD countries	**17.6**	**15.1**	**20.1**	**24.9**	**25.0**	**24.8**	**40.7**	**38.6**	**43.0**

Source: Education at a Glance, op. cit.

Table 5. **Number of enrolled students (full-time equivalents) in public and private tertiary education per 100 persons in the population in the typical age group, 1991**

(indicator P11)

	Non-university education			University education		
	M + W	Men	Women	M + W	Men	Women
Austria	**3.3**	**2.2**	**4.4**	**25.3**	**28.0**	**22.4**
Other EFTA						
Finland	31.4	21.9	41.2	26.5	26.9	26.1
Norway	40.5	38.5	42.7	21.9	19.9	24.0
Sweden	35.9	27.7	44.4	11.1	11.7	10.6
Switzerland	17.0	22.8	11.1	11.3	13.9	8.7
EU countries						
Belgium	19.3	15.0	23.8	13.1	14.8	11.2
Denmark	8.1	8.6	7.6	25.1	24.0	26.3

Source: Education at Glance, op. cit.

Table 6. **Ratio of first-degree graduates to 100 persons in the population at the theoretical age of graduation by gender, public and private universities, 1991**

(indicator R6)

	M + W	Men	Women
Austria	**7.8**	**8.5**	**7.0**
Other EFTA			
Finland	17.2	17.0	17.4
Norway	30.8	22.3	39.7
Sweden	12.0	10.4	13.6
Switzerland	7.6	9.8	5.4
EU countries			
Belgium	13.3	15.0	11.5
Denmark	16.5	14.4	18.7
Mean for all OECD countries	16.4	16.1	16.7

Source: Education at a Glance, op. cit.

Table 7. **Science and engineering degrees as a percentage of total university degrees by gender, public and private institutions, 1991**

(indicator R8, Table S16)

	M + W	Men	Women
Austria	**21.9**	**30.6**	**9.8**
Other EFTA			
Finland	33.2	52.1	12.7
Norway	16.5	28.7	7.5
Sweden	26.1	41.0	12.8
Switzerland	25.0	31.3	12.5
EU countries			
Belgium	32.2	–	–
Denmark	26.1	42.0	11.0
Mean for all OECD countries	22.5	32.1	11.2

Source: Education at a Glance, op. cit.

Table 8. **Engineering degrees as a percentage of total university degrees by gender, public and private institutions, 1991**

(indicator R7, Table S16)

	M + W	Men	Women
Austria	**10.3**	**16.6**	**1.6**
Other EFTA			
Finland	22.1	37.0	5.9
Norway	12.6	22.7	5.1
Sweden	17.0	28.7	6.5
Switzerland	7.8	11.1	1.2
EU countries			
Belgium	26.3	–	–
Denmark	18.8	31.5	6.7
Mean for all OECD countries	12.1	19.4	3.3

Source: Education at a Glance, op. cit.

The economy, employment and education

The Background Report bases its estimates on the economy's needs for skilled labour by the year 2000 on a *Wirtschaftsforschungsinstitut* (WIFO) scenario which assumes a growth rate of 3.2 per cent a year from 1990 to 1995 (justified by the efforts to catch up with the Western European countries) and 2 per cent between 1995 and 2000 (described as ''normal''). These estimates are supplemented by assumptions concerning hours worked and labour productivity, from which a forecast for total employment is deduced. This forecast is then broken down into 19 branches and, within each branch, into six ''qualification levels'' which are, in fact, educational attainment levels, from the completion of compulsory schooling to university graduation. We are obviously not able to judge the relevance of the economic scenario used, but we comment on issues which relate to higher education.

First, knowledge of the present employment situation by branch and qualification levels lacks precision. The last census was in 1981 and the results of the microcensuses conducted since then, particularly in 1989, are not comparable with the census data.

It seems that the forecasts for the years 1995 and 2000 were obtained simply by extrapolating trends in the distribution of economically active persons among the various educational levels in each branch between the 1971 and 1981 censuses. With this method, it is not possible to take into account what may be known about technological change, capital/labour substitution, productivity, changes in competition, etc., especially since the limited number of branches does not allow a detailed analysis. Without necessarily going so far as to use such refined forecasting models as those of the IAB (*Institut für*

Arbeitsmarkt und Berufsforschung der Bundesanstalt für Arbeit) in Germany or the Institute for Employment Research in the United Kingdom, the qualification structure in the initial period should probably be further disaggregated, particularly with regard to branches and an attempt made to adjust the trends observed by means of expert opinion where appropriate.

If the economically active population grows by 1.1 per cent a year from 1990 to 1995, and by 0.7 per cent a year from 1995 to 2000 as foreseen by WIFO, it will increase by 9.3 per cent over the entire period and therefore be roughly equivalent to the 3 609 500 given in the Background Report. Is this increase likely? Is it not somewhat optimistic considering the medium-term prospects for employment in Western countries? It is also to be noted that another forecast for employment by branch, also worked out by WIFO, refers to an insignificant increase of 0.1 per cent for the same period.

The list of qualifications used here shows the importance of formal qualifications in the Austrian social system, but there is no way of obtaining a picture of jobs by identifying the functions actually carried out within firms and government departments. According to the forecast, only those with lowest qualification level, "compulsory education", should decrease – by about 21 per cent – between 1990 and 2000. The numbers in all the other levels should rise:

University:	+27 per cent
BHS: higher technical/vocational secondary school	+32 per cent
AHS: higher general secondary school	+15 per cent
BMS: medium-level technical/vocational school	+35 per cent
Apprenticeship:	+18 per cent

Table 9.   **The age structure of the population: age groups 15-19 and 20-24**

(estimates and forecasts, 1990-2010)

	15-19			20-24		
	1990[1]	2000	2010	1990[1]	2000	2010
EFTA countries						
Austria	**6.6**	**6.0**	**5.8**	**8.2**	**5.7**	**5.8**
Finland	6.1	6.5	5.8	7.1	6.5	6.2
Norway	7.7	6.0	6.1	8.0	6.3	6.0
Sweden	6.6	5.1	6.3	7.0	5.8	6.5
Switzerland	6.2	5.1	5.8	7.6	5.6	5.9
EU countries						
Belgium	6.5	5.8	5.9	7.2	6.0	5.8
Denmark	7.2	5.4	5.6	7.7	6.2	5.5

1.   The figures for 1990 are estimates and the projections are based on the medium variant.
Source: The Sex and Age Distribution: The 1991 Revision of the United Nations Global Population Estimates and Projections, United Nations, New York, 1991.

Are such substantial changes in numbers really likely within the next ten years? In particular, the forecast increase for the BMS category (full-time, middle-level vocational education) of almost 180 000 seems out of the question since the number of students leaving these schools every year does not yet exceed 10 000. The forecasts in Table 9 show that nearly all the selected countries anticipate a decline in the 15-24 age group, particularly in the 20-24 age group as far as Austria is concerned.

Thus, these employment forecasts do not permit definite conclusions to be drawn on the future needs for a labour force with a post-secondary education. Forecasts for a period of less than ten years are of little help with a decision such as the creation of *Fachhochschulen,* which involves a type of education differing from the current forms of post-secondary education.

The survey conducted for OECD on the trend in graduate employment between 1985 and 1990 in a sample of firms provides information on other points. One of the surprising results of this survey is that growth in the number of graduates was particularly high in firms with fewer than 500 employees, and at a minimum in firms with 2 000 to 5 000 employees. Thirty per cent of graduates were recruited as replacements and 60 per cent to meet increased job requirements within firms. Growth in the number of graduates was high in the banking and insurance sector as well as the retail and wholesale trade sectors. The proportion of engineers declined in all branches, which shows that recruitment in the non-technical sectors predominated. Is it to be concluded, as does the author of the survey, that this decrease reflects a serious shortage of engineering graduates? This is impossible to determine without further information.

Chapter 4

REFORM IN HIGHER EDUCATION: UNIVERSITIES

Post-secondary education in Austria is characterised by a preponderance of academic rather than vocational education, since more than 80 per cent of tertiary beginners study at university institutions. There is widespread discussion of the need to improve this system. Current debate has focused on proposals for reform of university management. We detect a need for even more substantial reform of a wide range of aspects of the university system.

We believe that reform would be facilitated if there was a wider understanding of the functions of the higher education system and the university – and other institutions – within it. We suggest that there is need for broad public debate on these issues, to reformulate and preserve the essential functions of higher education. The reforms proposed in the "orange paper" have initiated this process; in our view, there is a need for discussion and action on a wider range of reforms. We make some suggestions for the framework of such a debate in Chapter 6.

Regional distribution

The geographical distribution of university institutions in Austria is uneven. There are twelve universities (the six colleges of art are not dealt with in this report). Of these twelve institutions, only the three founded several centuries ago (Vienna, Graz and Innsbruck) are complete universities, in the sense that they possess a classical structure. The two relatively new ones (Linz and Salzburg) cover fewer disciplines; the rest are specialised, two of them (the universities of Vienna and Graz) covering the field of technology.

About a third of the nearly 200 000 university students in Austria are registered at the oldest one, the University of Vienna. In addition, four of the specialised academic institutions are located in this same city, contrasting with the fact that only about 13 per cent of pupils in compulsory education attend schools in the capital. This concentration is a remnant of the time when Vienna was the political and geographical centre of a much larger empire and causes an imbalance in the educational opportunities offered by the different *Bundesländer*. The percentage of university students in the relevant age group varies considerably between Vienna and more distant *Bundesländer* without universities.

The universities supply not only higher *cadres* for the economy and the administration, but they are also the site for most of the research activity. They employ 40 per cent of all public and private research staff. This provides an essential basis for their manifold service functions (such as technical consultation to public bodies) which represents the third mission of modern universities. The lack of such institutions therefore has far-reaching consequences for a region.

Thus, there is a need for a better distribution of provision in higher education and future reforms should work towards this. To a certain extent this can be achieved by the presence of first-rate non-university establishments (such as *Fachhochschulen*). This can be combined with measures to ensure easy access to universities in other parts of the country.

Universities and the economy

A better interaction of the universities with the economy is recognised as an essential objective in European industrialised countries. The European Union has developed a special programme (COMETT) to promote this. The Austrian government is making a particular effort to encourage co-operation between the universities and the Austrian economy.

The declared objective of the coalition parties in the *Arbeitsübereinkommen der Regierung* is to increase private and public R&D expenditure so that its share of GDP corresponds to the OECD average. This has not yet been reached and will require further efforts in the coming years.

Initiatives to improve the transfer of knowledge to the economy have multiplied in the 1980s, for instance with the establishment of centres for the transfer of technologies and of outside stations of universities. Besides Austrian participation in COMETT II, there is a national scheme to detach scientific personnel from the universities to companies for up to two years.

Legal measures such as giving university establishments their own legal personality (as in the "Orange Paper") and allowing them to use income from outside contracts have considerably increased the attractiveness of research and consultancy. This permits the employment of additional personnel and the acquisition of special equipment which cannot be financed with the limited university budget. In 1987/88, 61 per cent of university institutes reported that they did contract research or acted as experts to the outside world.

In view of this figure, it is surprising that in 1991 only 8 per cent of university staff were financed by research income (including the subsidies given by the two funds for the promotion of research). This figure reflects the fact that only a comparatively modest amount of research money is available in Austria, since industry is in general not very research-minded and the government still spends relatively less on research than the governments of other industrially advanced countries, despite considerable progress in recent years.

Of course a large number of university graduates should be permanently employed by the economy. Despite the considerable growth of the student body, the corresponding "output" of the universities has not increased sufficiently to satisfy the needs in all professions. This situation is mainly caused by the high drop-out rates and the extremely long average duration of studies, and can be improved by reforms in teaching and other measures described below.

The development of closer links to the economy has created some concern in the university sector that this aligns academic activities too much with short-term utilitarian goals. The university should not be turned into a commercial enterprise but maintain its traditional role as a place where fundamental science and culture is fostered and transmitted as well as its long-range orientation. Even the modern mass university is not just a school for professional training and it would lose the essential support of the general public if it refused to respond to societal needs and to contribute to the solution of actual problems of human society. The university must recognise that the majority of the students are not interested in an academic career but want to obtain a sound practical basis for their future professional life. This will not essentially change even if *Fachhochschulen* relieve the university of a part of this majority.

The university thus has to strike a reasonable balance between its long-term mission, including in particular basic research, and its duty to offer an education which meets the demands of the labour market and to participate in coping with present problems, especially those of the economy. The public debate we propose, on the functions of the higher education system and the university and other institutions within it, would assist in formulating the function of the modern university in Austria.

Quality and efficiency of studies

Whilst, in the opinion of the "customers" of the university system, the quality of the output of university graduates – above all in industry – is satisfactory, the number of graduates is still insufficient in several fields. Major causes of this situation are the long duration of studies and the high drop-out rate among students. Only about half of them finish their studies with a degree and this usually happens after 7 to 9 years. In comparison with other OECD countries, such as the United Kingdom, where students often graduate from university at the age of 21-23, Austrian students tend to enter professional life three to five years later than their counterparts.

Several reasons are given for this unsatisfactory situation which together reflect some fundamental concerns about higher education. In the Austrian tradition, the universities do not have an explicit responsibility towards students for their academic advancement in the chosen curricula; as stated in the Background Report, the Humboldtian ideal emphasizes the acquisition of scientific knowledge by personal research performance. The central idea is the "training of the researcher". Academic staff often see their prime task as research, not teaching. The demands of the subject are paramount, not those of the student. Generally, students are expected to acquire knowledge not directed at particular vocations or professions, but of an academic subject. Insofar as students are educated for later professional life, it is a usually unstated assumption that this kind of learning will somehow be of value.

This reflects the historic structure of courses in Austrian universities and the failure of earlier reforms. Before the reforms of the 1960s, all students were enrolled in doctoral programmes, which were necessarily loosely structured. The reforms introduced the *Magister* award, intended as a preparation for vocational life. But the *Magister* is still seen as a preparation for the doctoral programme, and has thus a heavily overloaded curriculum. At the same time universities have expanded rapidly, and have been overloaded in other ways.

The high drop-out rate reflects a certain professorial aloofness stemming from the attitude which values research more than teaching. As one university academic put it: "if they (the government) want us to teach them (the students), they should pay for it". Achievements in research are usually more highly rewarded, not only financially, but also by other ways of public recognition; professors' pay is enhanced by the number of students taking examinations, not passing them; so there is little incentive to improve the standing of teaching in the universities.

The high student/teacher ratio affects the drop-out rate and length of studies. Between 1980 and 1990 the total number of students increased by 60 per cent whereas an estimate shows that the number of teaching hours per week offered by the university staff has grown merely by approximately 34 per cent during the same period.

The system of student support also contributes to the problems of Austrian universities. The material advantages accorded to students are apparently sufficient for some young people to enrol at a university although they have no intention to work seriously for a degree. Since they do not have to pay fees and there is no effective control of their academic progress, they can live quite happily, albeit modestly, in this way.

Furthermore students frequently earn money through part-time or even full-time jobs, so that they are able to devote only a limited effort to studying. In some cases they may be forced to do so, for example because they are already married and cannot claim enough social aid on the grounds that they come from middle-class families. This not only lengthens their study time but also increases the temptation to drop out because attention has to be split between too many obligations. A number of measures have been considered to improve these circumstances.

The "Orange Paper" on university reform proposed to create a dean for teaching in each faculty to co-ordinate the courses. In addition, a strategic body, the Commission for curricular matters (*Studienkommission*), would give general directives to the dean and decide on curricula. Thus teaching should attain higher attention within the university.

There is clearly a need to increase the responsibility and rewards of academic staff for teaching. One obvious method – to fix the salaries of the academic staff taking into account performance in teaching – may be difficult to apply because it requires evaluation of the teachers, including perhaps the judgement of their students. In the traditional universities, especially in the German-speaking countries, there is considerable opposition to giving students such influence, although this is common practice in countries such as the United States.

The increase of staff responsibility for teaching may lead to changes in the way professors transmit their knowledge and work with their students, thus increasing the efficiency of this process. Overcrowded universities, however, do not favour reforms away from the classical frontal instruction in big lecture halls, since these changes usually require a reasonably low student/teacher ratio. An increase in numbers of academic staff may help to shorten the duration of studies, but the universities would have to demonstrate a commitment to change in teaching methods before further funds would be released.

The introduction of fees has been proposed, at a level sufficiently high that registration would no longer be attractive to those who are not seriously interested in education. As noted earlier, we see the introduction of fees as almost inevitable in order to cope with financial requirements.

Another proposal would be a thorough reform of the assistance schemes for students so that they can more easily devote their time to studying. The *Studienförderungsgesetz 1992* (Act on Student Aid) brings considerable improvements, but it remains to be seen whether they are sufficient. We believe that such reform would in any case be necessary in parallel to any introduction of fees, in order to avoid discrimination against poorer candidates.

A further reform discussed in this context is the introduction of enforced rules for the length of the different phases of the curriculum. Prolongation should only be possible for valid reasons. An examination would have to be passed at the end of each phase and only one or two repetitions would be allowed in case of failure, in contrast to the three or more attempts currently permitted. Such rules would be preferable to restrictions on the duration of scholarships, which would put pressure only on the economically less favoured students.

Measures such as these obviously infringe on the existing generous right of individuals in Austria to free access to universities as long as they possess qualifications for the corresponding studies. To maintain this right costs sums that the federal government can no longer reasonably be expected to cover within a deficit budget. It might also appear questionable that the taxpayer's money should be so open-handedly used for a minority to enjoy the privilege of a stay at university without an obligation to prove that it really serves him or her to obtain a higher education within a reasonable time-frame.

The Austrian government has remarkably increased the share of the federal budget for the universities (including colleges of art and music) from 2.4 per cent in 1970 to 3.8 per cent in 1992. Whether this can continue at such a pace is not certain given the present financial situation. So, in absolute figures, the universities should not expect bigger governmental support in the coming years. Without the introduction of reforms, the quality of teaching at the university will probably deteriorate further. An alternative, or possibly an addition, to these reforms would be the introduction of a *numerus clausus,* with far-reaching consequences for the Austrian education system.

Up to now the higher secondary schools have been responsible for selecting and preparing young people for academic studies. Their leaving certificate, the *Matura,* gives them a right of admission to any faculty without further examination. A *numerus clausus* would require control at the entrance to the universities which could depreciate the value of this certificate. The alternative adopted by Germany to use the averages of the marks obtained in the high school leaving certificate as a selection criterion avoids this danger but it affects the objective of the high schools to offer a balanced all-round education. In a *numerus clausus* regime, many pupils choose their courses on the basis of how easy it is to obtain good marks, instead of being guided by the need for a well-balanced general education as a foundation for their future role in society. Some Austrian university professors prefer admission by an entrance examination administered by each faculty, as practised by elite universities in other OECD countries. This system may force the high school pupils to early specialisation to gain sufficient time for preparing themselves for the tests.

Research

Attributing a higher value to teaching should not lead to neglect research activity in Austrian universities. Research is essential to attract and retain a first-rate academic staff able to offer up-to-date instruction in their field. It also constitutes a training ground for those students who want to pursue a scientific career leading eventually to a chair in a university. In addition, it should allow Austria to participate in worldwide efforts to increase and improve human knowledge by basic research.

In recent years the government has made considerable efforts to improve the financial support available for academic research. The continuation of this policy is of prime importance for acquiring and maintaining the internationally recognised scientific reputation of Austrian universities. Of course, this represents only a necessary and not a sufficient condition because it requires innovative heads to use the available means in a creative way.

The unity of teaching and research is a fundamental principle prescribed legally by the *Universitätsorganisationsgesetz* (Act on the organisation of universities) of 1975. In the modern mass university, the implementation of this principle creates problems at undergraduate level where the numerous students to be taught require a large teaching staff. Considerable sums of money will be required if all staff are to engage in research. Without the proper, often expensive, equipment it is impossible to realise scientific investigations at the front-line of modern science.

In some OECD countries, big industrial companies assist with these requirements, either by giving outright grants or by drawing up paid contracts for specific projects. The Austrian industry, with a few notable exceptions, spends very little in this way: only about half of Austria's expenditures on R&D are financed by the economy and the main load for providing research funds at the universities remains with the federal government. In view of its current financial situation, the question "to what extent can the unity of teaching and research be maintained?" has to be examined carefully. There is no point spreading limited funds so that everybody receives some research money, since this would only lead to second-rate activities in this field.

Only two reasonable answers exist – either the number of students at the universities must be considerably reduced, or some members of the staff must limit their research activities. Probably only a combination of these two approaches will bring about more efficient use of the available research funds and a reduction in the growth of the student body of the universities.

In the first case, this means that attractive alternatives to a university education have to be offered in sufficient quantity and quality. This is the only way in which the growing need for higher education can be satisfied and the proposed *Fachhochschulen* could fulfil this function. Such a development also takes into account the fact that a majority of those who wish to obtain post-secondary education do not really intend to pursue an academic career. They are more interested in a professional training which gives them a good chance of employment. It should offer them the knowledge and the skills essential for performing efficiently in their future job. The academic foundations of subject disciplines, which according to the university laws represent the main topic of their curricula, matter less in such a context.

The second way of solving the problem would lead to an open recognition of the fact that excellence in research does not necessarily correlate with an outstanding performance in teaching and *vice versa*. It is important to distinguish between basic studies in the first part of the curriculum and the special studies of the second part, and of graduate study including the preparation for a doctoral degree. In the latter case, an intimate familiarity with the recent advances of research, best acquired by one's own activities, is essential for up-to-date instruction.

Often, first-year courses are taught by young assistants who possess limited research experience. Thus, the introduction of staff positions primarily for, or even restricted to, teaching would not fundamentally change the character of the university. But it could improve the quality of both teaching and research because it would allow better use of staff according to their abilities in teaching and research.

Some overall planning of university research is necessary for efficiency to be promoted. This should help to achieve a "critical mass" for important research at selected universities.

The *Forschungsorganisationsgesetz* (Act on the organisation of research) of 1981 created an Austrian Council for Science and Research to advise the ministries on science policy. In comparison with similar bodies in other countries (*e.g.* Germany or Switzerland) this body meets rather rarely. Thus, it has only a modest influence on the planning and co-ordination of academic research. So these tasks are left to a considerable extent to the BMWF, which means a top-down approach. The experiences of other countries show that an active participation of research workers is essential for effective co-ordination and realistic planning. The development of research in Austria should not be determined almost entirely by the appointments of teaching staff at the universities. In any case, such appointments should be made in the context of a national research policy.

Deregulation for the universities

Increasing the responsiveness of the universities requires substantial changes in the legal framework governing their operation. The changes required challenge the traditional detailed central regulation of higher education.

There are an impressive number of laws and ordinances governing the universities in a very detailed way. The Austrian lawmakers have done their utmost to formulate clear regulations for all aspects of the university and of its activities. The remarkable uniformity of these institutions seems to have an advantage at least on paper. For instance, students who wish to transfer from one university to the other can do so without difficulty. To the outsider however the question "to what extent is reality fully in accordance with the intricate net of legal requirements?" comes up. In all likelihood, few people master all the intricacies of the legal requirements concerning the universities. As a consequence the real world of the university sometimes does not always develop in absolute conformity with the law.

The complexity of university legislation is exemplified by the legal prescriptions regulating university studies which comprise two law and ordinance levels. The basic law on studies at universities (*allgemeines Hochschulsstudiengesetz,* AHSTG) of 1966 defines general prescriptions for matriculation and admission, the structure and organisation of studies, the form and implementation of examinations as well as the award of academic degrees. In addition, it assigns regulating authority to the special study laws, study orders and study plans, the three other subordinated levels.

For brevity's sake, only the contents of the special study laws are outlined here. They define, for a course or group of courses, the curricula and possibly their subdivision in study branches, the number of study phases, their minimal length, the subjects of the diploma and other examinations, the organisation of the examinations and the academic degrees and designations for the corresponding professions.

Bringing changes to all these laws is time-consuming, involving consultation with all interested bodies, yet changes in the laws are increasingly required. The AHSTG was revised five times in the last decade, which constitutes a remarkable achievement given the cumbersome procedures for passing such legislation.

The subject of descriptive geometry furnishes a striking example of the difficulties involved in this system of detailed legal regulation. This subject does no longer exist in technical universities such as the Swiss Federal Institute of Technology because of the widespread use of computers for designing (known as CAD). Yet, according to Austrian law, this is still a required subject for the first diploma of civil and mechanical engineers. The law helps to protect some university teachers in outdated fields but hampers quick adaptations to new situations.

The treatment of such matters on the political level allows interested groups outside the university to influence regulations. But it is also possible to ensure such a participation if authority is given to a professionally competent body which can work with considerably streamlined procedures. Such a change could also help to increase the autonomy of the universities.

University autonomy

Measures to increase autonomy formed part of the proposals for university reform in the "green paper" and the "orange paper". They concentrated on an organisational reform to reshape and reinforce the different university bodies by transferring to them a number of responsibilities from the BMWF. The following discussion relates to the position at the time of the examiners' visit, before the issues raised by the consultation process were incorporated in the draft law.

A clear division of functions and responsibilities between different levels, viz. the institutes or departments, the faculty, and the whole institution was proposed. An executive vested with adequate powers and responsibility was proposed for each level. The strategic and co-ordinating function was to be exercised by commissions, in which the staff and the students are represented. The executive body at the head of the university would be enlarged to at least one rector and three vice-rectors, all full-time and with more managerial tasks than the present mainly representative duties.

The university would obtain far-reaching control of its budget, since all expenditures would be integrated in one budgetline of the federal budget, the distribution of which would be left to the university. There would be no separation of the costs for personnel and supplies, so that the management would have flexibility in using available financial resources.

But such a change, which many universities in other OECD countries would like to obtain, is not greeted with great enthusiasm in Austrian universities. If members of the university decide on the distribution of the sum allotted by the federal government and the parliament, the fear exists that they would use this power too much in their own interests or spread the money too widely to avoid hard decisions. In the eyes of university staff, the federal ministries are better suited for this task.

Many of the other proposals in the reform have been criticised, although the BMWF has already taken into account a number of suggestions to change its original concept. For instance, there is strong opposition among the university staff to the idea that the rector and vice-rectors should be elected by the "university assembly" from a list proposed by a commission consisting half and half of members nominated by the senate and the BMWF – which also appoints its chairman. In this case, the intervention of the Ministry is rejected as a threat to autonomy. We do not see why a university cannot elect its own rector. But in general the statements from university bodies on the reform betray the desire to maximise the autonomy of individual departments or sometimes even the individual professor beyond what is acceptable on the political level.

Outside the university, for example in the federal administration, it is feared that this new concept no longer allows the government to realise a concerted science policy. There is a way to reduce or eliminate this danger by setting aside "earmarked" funds within the budget of the BMWF, which would be reserved for specific projects designed to achieve particular policy aims. Thus, the Ministry could restrict its role to determining the global goals and the overall planning and organisation, with the exception of these instruments for direct intervention.

Academic personnel at the university

The reform of universities also necessitates re-examination of the traditional functions of academic staff. The situation of academic personnel in university institutions has gradually evolved, from a strongly hierarchical system headed by a chairholder, usually a full professor, to one with fairly broad participation of all groups of employees. Thus, assistants are selected by the relevant commission of academic personnel. Such a procedure gives little opportunity to individuals to choose their own staff.

In contrast to this, the right to teach is not yet the same for all of those who are involved in this activity. Only those who have passed the "Habilitation" possess full authority to teach (*venia docendi*). Yet about two-thirds of the teaching is done by the assistants or lecturers without *venia docendi,* who are given only an auxiliary role by the law.

The authority to teach also determines other rights such as being an examiner, guiding scientific work and using equipment. Since a large share of the teaching load is assumed by the intermediary staff, the reality is obviously somewhat different from what the law suggests.

The responsibility for deciding the appointments of senior academic personnel is the prerogative of the BMWF Minister; this is in contradiction with the management principle according to which such decisions should be taken by those who are directly concerned. The "orange paper" proposal – that a commission for each academic unit composed of representatives of different groups of staff should elect all those employed at this unit with the exception of professors – would be more in line with these principles.

The academic staff of the universities is rather static in its composition, in contradiction with the highly dynamic development of science and with the environment of these institutions. All professors enjoy permanent appointments as tenured civil servants and the yearly turnover of assistants amounts to a mere 10 per cent of the total. The modest increase of the number of positions with the status of civil servant in the last decade (only 3 per cent for ordinary professors, 11 per cent for assistants and 9 per cent for all university teachers) could not seriously alleviate this problem. In addition, there is a problem of "inbreeding", in the sense that many staff are graduates of one university and stay there for practically all their academic career.

It has also been proposed to appoint some professors only for a limited time, with the possibility of prolongation if this proves to be mutually desirable. This would allow increased flexibility, and reduce the inertia of the universities preventing adaptation to changed circumstances.

The managerial reforms proposed by the government, and the continuing need to reform university curricula and teaching, will place heavy demands on academic personnel. Experience from other OECD countries shows that these should not be underestimated. There will be a need for considerable administrative support for the universities if they are to exercise their proposed managerial responsibilities, and a need for training and development of managerial skills for academic staff. There will be a need for a programme of staff development to assist university staff in taking a more active part in the generation of new teaching methods and curricula.

Co-ordination between the universities

The delegation of important powers from the Ministry to the individual universities increases the importance of co-ordination between the institutions. The "Orange Paper" proposed a special body, the *Universitäten-Kuratorium,* responsible for national planning and co-ordination. We see this serving an important function as a buffer between universities and provinces. Among its major tasks would be the elaboration of a national development plan for a four-year period, the allotment of the global budgets to each university (taking into account the amount available for this purpose in the budget of the Ministry as well as the directives of the Minister) and the overall evaluation of the universities. The national development plan should represent a synthesis of the corresponding plans of each university and furnish the basis for the annual budgetary requests of the BMWF.

These proposals compare favourably with the corresponding arrangements of other OECD countries. The only major shortcoming is in the field of research planning. The orange paper does not mention explicitly how the national development plan is linked with the planning based on the overall research concept for the 1990s which is under preparation, and in particular with the plans of the two funds for the promotion of research. Because of the central role which the universities play in the Austrian research effort, there should be close coupling between the co-ordination of the universities and of research activities. In this context the mandate of the Austrian Council for science and research should be re-examined.

The implementation of the proposals in the orange paper would increase the number of commissions active in the field of university and research policy. The question arises of whether this proliferation could not be reduced by merging some of them, thus reducing the need for co-ordination.

Continuing education at the university

The Austrian government has already created the legal basis for continuing education in universities and the universities have developed a considerable variety of offers for continuing education which is nowadays a must for practically all their graduates.

However, they have not approached this responsibility in a systematic way so that there are serious gaps. In particular in fields of small economic interest, their offer is quite inadequate. The overload caused by the large number of undergraduate students wanting to obtain a first education is no doubt a good excuse for this.

Continuing education has become essential for maintaining the professional qualifications required on the labour market, and the universities should obtain more means to create and maintain an efficient infrastructure and a competent organisation for courses and other activities in this field. It is difficult, if not impossible, to meet these needs only by an appendix to the curricula of initial education.

Austria has already realised the possibility of using distance education for this purpose, and for second-chance education, by concluding a contract with the Distance

University of Hagen in Germany. In many fields, such as mathematics and sciences, it is possible to use German teaching material. But there are other subjects such as history and law for which Austria should develop its own material to maintain its cultural and political identity. The existing universities offer an appropriate framework to realise such a contribution going beyond just operating simple satellites of Hagen and should receive governmental support for this.

Chapter 5

REFORM IN HIGHER EDUCATION:
VOCATIONAL EDUCATION AND THE FACHHOCHSCHULEN

Vocational training: present arrangements

The Austrian vocational education system, like the rest of the system, is character-ised by certain features which may be summed up in two words: quality and elitism.

Quality is achieved in part by the ability and commitment of the teaching and administrative staff, but simple funding also helps. OECD comparative statistics for 1991 (Table 1) show that, at that time, Austria reached exactly the OECD country mean (5.4 per cent) in terms of public education expenditure related to GDP. It was preceded only by the Nordic countries. Public spending per secondary pupil ($4 680) was higher than the OECD country mean ($4 179) (OECD, 1993, indicator P6). The average number of pupils per teacher was among the lowest: 10.8 in primary education, 6.7 in the lower cycle and 10.0 in the secondary education as a whole. These averages were substantially lower than those in Germany and lower by about half than those recorded in France (OECD, 1993, indicator P10).

Some 1991 figures underline characteristics of the Austrian system. The enrolment in upper secondary education at 86.6 per cent ranks Austria higher than the OECD country mean (79.3 per cent) and before North American countries, France, the Netherlands and Sweden in terms of the number of upper secondary graduates per 100 persons in the population at the theoretical age of graduation. These data should be read in conjunction with the comparative performances in Tables 4 and 6 of first entrants to tertiary education and the ratio of first degree graduates. These figures are a result of two main factors: first, a process of early selection, like the one used in Germany, in which the teaching staff play a major role and which takes place in two phases, at ages 10 and 14; secondly, they are the result of restricting university entrance to pupils who have passed the *Matura,* the university having a quasi-monopoly in tertiary education. In the latter two examples quoted above, Austria is far from reaching either the OECD country mean or the levels of comparable countries, except for first entrants to university educa-tion. It should be recalled that (according to Table A.3 in Annex 2 of Part One) around 42 per cent of upper secondary students were enrolled in streams preparing for the *Matura.* This selection system has long been criticised for being a way of maintaining the social hierarchy of the past, rather than for guiding young people into the kinds of training and jobs in which they could develop their abilities. That the consultations on the diversification project for higher education have rekindled this controversy is not surprising. OECD reports have already expressed some misgivings on this selection policy.

Secondary education, and particularly its upper cycle, is a closely regulated and complicated system, with five types of schools – some of which include a number of streams. The system is highly segmented: once a pupil enters a stream it is very difficult to change and this is practically impossible in the upper cycle. Information for young people on training possibilities and jobs is also reported to leave much to be desired. In any case, it is difficult to give guidance for such a complex and rigid system.

There are two different levels of school in vocational training – higher schools (BHS) and medium-level (BMS) schools. The difference between them is seen mainly in the ability of the pupils admitted. The number of pupils in the higher-level schools is rising quickly, while those in the medium level schools are stable or are starting to decrease slightly.

The higher secondary vocational schools (BHS) provide the best educational opportunities as they lead to the *Matura* and therefore to university and to working life. But the course is long and exacting. The BHS takes five years instead of the four years of higher secondary general schools (AHS) which also lead to the *Matura*. Furthermore, the BHS has very full syllabuses and heavy timetables of about 40 hours a week. The training is sound, practical and appreciated by employers, despite limitations. Some even go so far as to claim that BHS diplomas are almost on a par with the French BTS (*baccalauréat* + two years) or even the German FHS (*Abitur* + three years). However, this view is not really tenable and may cause some confusion in Europe since BHS-holders officially become engineers after three years of professional activity in their particular field, whereas Brussels requires three years of post-secondary education for recognition of this qualification. The BHS diploma-holders have none to their credit – unless their fifth year is accepted as the equivalent of a post-secondary year or unless it actually becomes a post-secondary year. This is a basic issue in connection with the setting up of *Fachhochschulen*.

A question of the same kind arises in connection with the *Kollegs*. Although the Austrian education system can often be criticised for its excessive segmentation, it must be given credit for devising through the *Kolleg* an original scheme for supplementing general education with technical training and therefore for bridging a gap which is generally ignored. Although training in these *Kollegs* is post-secondary since it is for AHS *Maturanten* (pupils with a general higher school-leaving certificate), it is provided on two-year BHS courses and reportedly gives such students a technical qualification comparable to that of the BHS *Matura* in addition to their wider general education, therefore ensuring very good opportunities for access to the labour market. The normal duration of the course from the end of the first cycle is thus six years or a year more than for the BHS certificate-holders.

The BMS, the middle-level vocational school, has a four-year course and does not lead to the *Matura,* and thus has an almost inevitably negative image, *i.e.* a school which is reserved for pupils who are neither wanted by the AHS and BHS nor interested in an apprenticeship. This image, which is supposed to be quite widespread among parents, is perhaps over-simplified, and it may be quite inaccurate in rural areas where not all types of schools are close at hand. In reality, the majority of pupils educated in these medium-level schools are not failures, as they have acquired a technical qualification that will enable them to find a job quite easily. Some of them then take advantage of the so-called *zweiter Bildungsweg* (second-chance education) which, by means of evening courses, allows them to go on to the *Matura* and, possibly, to higher education, whether at university or not. It must be admitted that this is a long road and that the number of those who manage to keep going until the end seems to be very small.

The apprenticeship scheme

The apprenticeship scheme plays an important part in vocational training since, after compulsory education, about 40 per cent of young people opt for this stream. It leads to a manual or non-manual worker's qualification that is – theoretically – the same as the one obtained at the full-time, medium-level apprenticeships as for BMS courses. However, four times as many young people opt for apprenticeships as for BMS courses.

The apprenticeship system is similar to that in Germany and Switzerland. The firm recruiting the apprentice plays the major role, while general and theoretical training is mainly part-time; examinations are held under the responsibility of the Chambers of Commerce and the federal government supervises the entire system. As in Germany and other countries, the employer and trade unions associations have a part to play, and their views often differ, particularly about the amount of time spent in school and in the firm, or the grouping of trades.

Although we were not able to study the apprenticeship scheme in detail, our findings suggest that the scheme does not play the same role in vocational training as it does in Germany and especially that it is less important. First, it is to be noted that several types of apprenticeship with differing characteristics come under the same regulations, *i.e.* those concerning:

- traditional arts and crafts and shopkeeping;
- technical trades (building trades, car repairs, etc.);
- trades in major industrial sectors.

Although regional particularities might suggest a slightly different picture than is given in this brief analysis, it seems that mainly the first two categories, in which individual firms are strongly represented and an apprenticeship is still the usual way of entering working life, are confronted with recruitment problems, since the number of apprenticeship vacancies far exceeds the number of applications. On the other hand, the apprenticeship seems to be much less of a tradition in major industrial firms than in Germany where it has so far provided access to all industrial trades, including those with a high technological content. In Austria, many industrial firms keep the number of apprentices low, or even no longer use the apprenticeship scheme, either because they consider that it is too costly or because they are not satisfied with the standard of applicants and prefer to recruit young people leaving the BMS, even if they need more time to get accustomed to factory life.

Accordingly, it may be asked if today's apprentices include young people who wish to go on to difficult post-secondary studies and are capable of doing so. Apprenticeship recruitment standards have probably deteriorated for a number of years compared with the school streams. Admittedly, the apprenticeship scheme is at a disadvantage since it is considered to be a dead end and, for age reasons, does not accept students until after completion of the pre-vocational *polytechnischer Lehrgang* year; some candidates see this year as having little justification and try to avoid it by crowding into the first year of the BHS and the BMS.

If a policy to improve the standards and prestige of the apprenticeship scheme were to be initiated, it seems to us that one step should be to make the scheme more attractive by eliminating the delay caused by the preparatory year and by organising simpler and clearer paths between school streams and apprenticeships than the present narrow bridges. Such a policy should give apprentices with the best track records possibilities of going further, and particularly on to the *Fachhochschulen*. Those who have done well on the most difficult apprenticeship courses might be admitted directly, while others might need further preparation. This could be at evening school, or on a full-time basis, provided that the ex-apprentices who would then have no income received maintenance grants.

The modernisation of the apprenticeship system should also include more general and theoretical training and provide for some groupings among the 225 trades taught in order to develop a multi-skilled and adaptable labour force. This modernisation probably requires some flexibility in the regulations so that greater allowance can be made for the range of apprenticeships and their particular requirements. Employers and trade unions are now arguing about the principle of such reforms, which is perhaps partly due to their habit of seeing the apprenticeship system as a single entity and of applying identical rules to heterogeneous components that would have to be treated differently.

Continuing training

The more efficient a country's initial vocational training, the more difficult it can be to recognise the need for continuing training and to develop it. In Austria, the idea that there is a time for acquiring knowledge and skills, if possible by obtaining formal qualifications, and a time for using this knowlege professionally, does not yet seem to be out of date. Those who believe that teachers should not simply pass on set knowledge, but also believe that some of this knowledge is perishable and that the training process should go on indefinitely, still have some difficulty in making their point.

Continuing training is, however, by no means inexistent. Employers realise the need for further training in the interests of both the firm and the workforce, and provide a certain amount of resources for it, either by organising internal training or by enabling employees to take part in outside courses, such as those organised by the Chambers of Commerce. On its side, the Ministry of Labour is responsible for training the unemployed and the Provincial Employment Departments organise an efficient system of "second chance" training, allowing adults to obtain an apprenticeship certificate within a year. (It is to be noted that this type of training is a new kind of apprenticeship leading to broad-based trades.) However, such action by the authorities seems to be limited to the initial level of professional qualifications. Neither the BHS schools nor the universities we visited seemed to be particularly interested in further training; they tend rather to leave this field to private bodies, even if their teaching staff work in a personal capacity with these bodies.

Continuing training, particularly for engineers, technicians and managers who have acquired a few years of professional experience, is therefore still patchy, segmented, not well organised and without an overall response to current and foreseeable needs. The system seems to lack stamina. We met nobody who felt really responsible for giving it a boost and promoting it throughout the country or in a province. In addition, the system reflects the segmentation of initial training, and saddles itself unnecessarily with the distinctions between the secondary and post-secondary phases of the initial system.

The development of continuing training should, it seems to us, be based on a sound distance training system benefitting from the experience of countries which are familiar with these techniques and covering if possible quite a wide range of training fields and levels. The country's geographical characteristics are another reason for using this method.

The *Fachhochschulen*

When the examiners visited Austria, a broadly-based consultation on a first draft of a *Fachhochschule* law was in its final stages. Although it confirmed mostly positive attitudes towards the introduction of this new type of institution, this proposal encountered opposition on numerous points of detail.

There is wide agreement within Austria on the need for a new form of post-secondary education in *Fachhochschulen*. There is particularly strong support from employers and others outside the education system; there is also, generally, support for such a sector from the universities. The need for a new form of education, vocationally oriented, and of about three years duration, is generally accepted.

It is accepted that the Austrian economy needs young technical personnel with a reasonably short post-secondary education. The universities have not been able to satisfy this demand although they are allowed to introduce short-cycle studies. A similar development has already taken place in other Western European countries such as Belgium, the Netherlands and Norway and is also under consideration in Switzerland, Austria's neighbouring country. The Austrian authorities intend to designate the planned new institutions in this sector as *Fachhochschulen* following the German example in this respect.

The creation of *Fachhochschulen* will affect without any doubt the existing universities. In the long run it will reduce the number of university students. If this will take away some of the pressures on the universities, the existence of *Fachhochschulen* may increase others. In particular their example may force the universities to improve their educational offers, so that, for instance, the present high drop-out rate is lowered.

An innovation at post-secondary level will also provoke a number of changes within secondary education. Institutions such as the 5-year BHS which extend into the third level have to find an appropriate arrangement with the corresponding *Fachhochschulen*. Either their graduates should receive recognition for their additional year of study when they start at a *Fachhochschule,* or their curricula should be shortened to four years.

The establishment of the *Fachhochschulen* should cause a systematic examination of the place and role of all the institutions which have been created in the past on an *ad hoc* basis for professional training. The great diversity described in the Background Report renders comparisons with school systems of other countries at times rather difficult. A clear framework for non-university institutions would make it possible to reshape the education system so that there would be less overlap between the secondary and post-secondary level. In an integrated Europe, this does not represent a mere formal improvement but contributes to the acceptance of Austrian education in other countries of the common economic space.

At present, the opposition to change affecting the existing educational institutions seems to be caused at least partially by the fear that vested interests may be lost under the new circumstances. In the opinion of the examiners, a greater readiness to enter into an interesting venture, even if it carries some risks for one's own position, is required in order to realise the basic changes essential for overcoming existing weaknesses. The systematic introduction of *Fachhochschulen* is not only essential for equilibrating the post-secondary system but also for trying out a new paradigm to overcome some of the present weaknesses in this sector.

The *Fachhochschulen* in relation to social and economic needs

The proposals for the reform of higher education and for developing the hitherto limited non-university sector by creating short, professionally-oriented courses based on the *Fachhochschule* model are intended to modernise and improve the efficiency of these types of education while bringing them into line, so to speak, with "European" standards. In developed countries as a whole, the demand for new skills combined with the aspiration for long courses of study from which advantages are expected in terms of jobs, remuneration and social status, is resulting in a general rise in educational levels. Austria knows that it cannot ignore this development, especially since its economic structure gives it few decisive assets in the field of competition. In the light of future social developments, this seems to be the right time to think more about the educational needs of the next fifteen years.

As the incorporation in the education system of institutions such as the *Fachhochschulen* has been discussed in Austria for a number of years, the main actors in the economy and interest groups have been able to think about the issue, discuss it and state their positions. They are not indifferent to the matter, and we noted very wide if not unanimous support for the principle of reform. Employers and trade unions, the management of major firms and the representatives of small and medium enterprises all seem to agree that the creation of *Fachhochschulen* will contribute to competitiveness and economic progress, even if they do not see eye to eye on the methods of implementing the project. This agreement in principle does not seem to have been challenged either by the main political parties or by the provincial governments.

The needs of firms

The main reason why employers say they are in favour of *Fachhochschulen* is that they need new types of skills which include sound theoretical knowledge and a concern with practical problems. Not that employers are starting to look down on the high-level technical/vocational schools (BHS). On the contrary, these are still appreciated and, in both engineering and business studies, still provide a high proportion of company management staff. It is considered that BHS engineers (five years of secondary technical school + three years of professional experience) are of a standard perfectly adequate for most production departments. Moreover, the demand for them abroad is such that there is talk of a brain drain to Germany and Switzerland. However, the limits inherent to their training are recognised: these engineers do have a speciality, but it is often relatively limited, and they seldom have the wide range of skills increasingly required, such as the combination of an engineering qualification with some knowledge of organisation, management, computer technology, and foreign languages.

University graduates are employed by firms in scientific and technical, commercial, administrative, legal and management posts. Apart from the fact that these graduates usually cannot be recruited until they are around 27 to 30 due to the length of their studies, they are often said to be more attracted by theory than practice. Their university education is said to encourage them to opt for research or design work rather than the down-to-earth activities of manufacturing, production, or managing the personnel responsible for coping with the daily incidents and surprises in the running of a factory or a department. It must be noted, though, that a significant proportion of graduates are in the public sector and that a large number of them are in fact teachers.

There is therefore a need for a different form of education, in terms of both age and skills. There can be no question of producing graduates whose university courses have simply been shortened or diluted. We do not consider that the many young people who leave university after a few years without a qualification can meet this need. Equally, the *Fachhochschule* graduates needed by the economy would have a practical, operational-style training developed beyond the BHS formula, including a wider theoretical basis that would ensure their adaptability and understanding of their speciality's complementary aspects.

As in many other countries, there is talk in Austria of "shortages of skilled labour", but it is quite difficult to form a precise idea of the nature, extent and causes of this, particularly in the case of staff with a higher education. Employers seem to have some difficulty in recruiting the engineers and high-level technicians they require to meet the increasing technical complexity of their industries. This need is especially felt in the technical field and manufacturers frequently criticise the education system for not reacting quickly enough to change. Some firms are now recruiting graduates from the German *Fachhochschulen,* and it can be assumed that they would be only too willing to take on nationals with a type of training that was similar or even better suited to their needs. We were struck by the very strong commitment to *Fachhochschulen* which we observed in the Vorarlberg region, an industrially dynamic province open to both Switzerland and Baden-Württemberg, the latter being so to speak the homeland of the *Fachhochschulen.* By and large, employers seem to be convinced that employees at a certain level of responsibility must have broader general education than those graduating from BHS currently possess.

The first signs of expectations, if not of demand, on the part of employers can therefore already be seen, and there are some reasons for thinking that this demand will increase in small and medium firms as well as in major enterprises as soon as there is a certain number of such graduates. In similar circumstances, supply has often had a positive influence on demand.

The Background Report contains an interesting study on the potential demand for *Fachhochschulen* which differentiates between categories of population concerned and the types of decision that might be involved. The estimated potential falls within an extremely wide range – 24 000 and 60 000 students in the initial year – but this is inevitable since the list of *Fachhochschule* courses and the entrance requirements for the various categories of candidates have not been worked out. As stressed by the Report, the estimate of numbers depends on many additional variables. Market research has still to be carried out.

If, as we think should be the case, a *Fachhochschule* education is not a shortened or diluted form of university education but one that differs in its emphasis, methods and teaching staff, it should also develop among its students aptitudes that are sometimes neglected by the present system. Some young people with AHS or BHS qualifications who enrol at university and then drop out could succeed in the new courses. This could also be the case for young people who are not ungifted but cannot attend university.

We asked employers, trade unionists and civil servants in various government departments about the social problems which might arise with the inclusion of a new category of employees – *Fachhochschulen* graduates – in the company hierarchy, taking existing collective agreements into account. Although the answers were sometimes evasive, we did not feel that major difficulties and potential conflicts were to be expected. The partners seem to be preparing for pragmatic solutions at branch or enterprise level. However, trade union representatives are closely following developments and are asking the right questions: How will young people from different school streams obtain places in *Fachhochschulen*? What will happen to those who have served an apprenticeship? How will their practical experience be taken into account? Exactly what kind of diploma will be awarded? What will be the possibilities of further training?

The trade unions to which the engineers/technicians belong are somewhat apprehensive about the potential competition from *Fachhochschulen* graduates, but at the same time they are aware of the possibilities of promotion for their members. They are not opposing the reform but trying to obtain assurances and guarantees on how it is to be implemented. It seems obvious to us that not only these engineers/technicians but also the other certified BHS students should be able to go on to the *Fachhochschule* by means of further training.

Young people and the *Fachhochschulen*

We had limited opportunity to discuss the proposed *Fachhoschulen* policy with students, but most students seem to be in favour of the creation of *Fachhochschulen*. This impression was confirmed in our meetings with the representatives of student unions. They were critical of the university system, which they describe as "the most complicated in Europe", of lack of guidance for newcomers and, generally speaking, of the inertia shown by the government and the universities with regard to the rise in student numbers. They support the creation of *Fachhochschulen* and consider them as different in theory and practice from universities. In particular, they believe that the creation of *Fachhochschulen* could help to reduce drop-out. Enrolment fees are admittedly a sensitive issue, especially since they are a threat to a free university education. Our impression is, however, that the principle of moderate enrolment fees, combined with appropriate financial assistance in both the FHS and the universities, does not really justify a call to arms.

Implementing the *Fachhochschule* policy

The draft law for the *Fachhochschulen* is a particularly innovative proposal in Austrian education. It attempts to do more than simply create a new set of institutions; it offers a way of doing so that breaks with the traditional heavily centralised and regulated Austrian model. We believe that it offers the opportunity to develop new approaches to tackle some of the systemic problems identified in Austrian policy-making in education. It is an important step in developing mechanisms for the deregulation and decentralisation that are widely held to be necessary for Austria's future well-being in a changing Europe.

The policy to establish *Fachhochschulen* has a number of important features that contribute to these ends. We believe that these essential features of the *Fachhochschule* policy must be retained if it is to be effective.

The accreditation model

The model of accreditation proposed for the *Facchhochschulen* is a particularly important element of the policy. It offers a new way of maintaining quality in the curriculum, of promoting innovation in curricula and in teaching methods. It offers a way of exercising these functions without the centralisation and detailed regulation that have characterised Austrian education. It is a model for deregulating quality control. We believe that it is essential for Austria to take this opportunity to pioneer decentralisation and deregulation.

The model offers the opportunity to eliminate detailed regulation of curricular content. The criteria of the *Fachhochschulrat* should be statements of the general rather than specific requirements of courses, identifying, for example, characteristics of the appropriate level, the need to ensure breadth of coverage and depth of study in particular subjects without prescribing content. They will place obligations on the *Fachhochschulen* to justify the nature of proposed courses, choice of content, methods of study, etc. Whilst the draft law contains rather more details on curricular matters than we would wish, which it will be more difficult to change than *Fachhochschulrat* regulations, it undoubtedly takes the opportunity to substantially deregulate curriculum content.

The creation of the *Fachhochschulrat* as a separate body for quality control also offers a way of decentralising quality control. It, not the Ministry, will have this responsibility, and the *Fachhochschulen* will be responsible for their own academic development. They will have to demonstrate that their courses meet the general criteria prescribed by the *Fachhochschulrat*.

An important feature of the model is that it separates academic and political decisions. It locates reponsibility for *educational* decisions within the academic community, *i.e.* the *Fachhochschulrat* and the educational institutions. For this reason, the fact that it is broadly composed of people with educational expertise, rather than representatives of sectional or political interests, is appropriate. Decisions on other aspects of the *Fachhochschulen*, such as funding, location, etc., are not academic decisions and the responsibility for them is located elsewhere.

The specification of the function of the *Fachhochschulrat* should be emphasized here. The *Fachhochschulrat* does not decide which institutions or courses will be funded (neither does it approve courses in institutions which cannot demonstrate security of funding). The responsibility for the national pattern of *Fachhochschule* education has *not* been removed from the government. The Minister also has reserve powers in the revised draft law to intervene if *Fachhochschulen* act illegally and to protect the national interest.

The draft law to create a *Fachhochschulrat* has generated a number of objections from different sectors of Austrian society and the education system. Some of these arise from the novel nature of the proposal in the Austrian context, seeking as it does to reduce the traditional reliance on ministerial control and regulation. Some of them arise from a misunderstanding of what is proposed. A number of the responses to the draft, whilst supporting the idea of a *Fachhochschule* sector, propose conditions and amendments that appear to be designed to frustrate its establishment. We believe that the government will be able to accommodate many of the objections to the draft. Many can be resolved by minor amendments.

Difficulties such as these are inevitable because this proposal constitutes a radically new approach to policy. An essential feature of the draft law is that it is concerned with establishing procedures, rather than with the traditional emphasis on content and resources. Here, it is important to remember that the law is only *part* of the *Fachhochschule* policy. Some of the responses to the draft complain that it does not discuss the detail of funding of the proposed *Fachhochschulen*, nor of their internal organisation and management, that it does not prescribe precise curricula through regulation. This is, of course, the point of this law. Funding and other matters are to be considered by the proposed *Fachhochschulrat* only insofar as they relate to its purpose as a quality control mechanism. Curricula are to be designed by the new institutions, and accredited only if they meet general criteria to be prescribed by the new body.

The draft law cannot however be considered in isolation. There is a need for the government to clarify its plan for funding of the *Fachhochschulen,* the proposed pattern of provision, and whether governmental or parliamentary regulations will be needed over their management. If such a plan had been published at the same time as the draft law, it might have allayed some of the criticisms.

Student progress

The *Fachhochschule* policy embodies the principle that the *Fachhochschulen* have a responsibility for the progress of their students. This contrasts with the implicit tradition in the universities already noted in Chapter 4, where the students, by and large, have to fend for themselves in matters of choice of course and academic progress. A number of factors should contribute to this. The *Fachhochschulen* will be designing courses with the future employment of their graduates in mind; they will select students. We believe they should develop the tradition we observed in higher vocational secondary institutions of helping these students to attain the educational and practical standards required for successful completion.

The task of ensuring that this principle is acknowledged in *Fachhochschulen* will rest with the *Fachhochschulrat* when it considers courses for accreditation. The *Fachhochschulen* will have to satisfy the *Fachhochschulrat* that they have procedures to meet these requirements. The provisions in the draft law for offering a record of achievement to students who do not complete courses should also help to promote this responsibility, and it will be useful to monitor the extent to which students and employers find this helpful.

Access

It is essential that the *Fachhochschulen* should offer routes to higher education to students from all the different streams in secondary education. They should increase the permeability of the education system, particularly for those who have entered the "dual system".

A corollary of this principle is that the *Fachhochschulen* should take account of the different educational backgrounds of their students. There will be a need for different kinds of provision for students from the "dual system", those from the 5-year BHS course and those from general secondary education. Again, it may be wise to abstain from prescribing precise curricula at the central level. The issue is better dealt with by the *Fachhochschulrat,* requiring *Fachhochschulen* to demonstrate how they propose to ensure entry to their courses by students from these different routes. They will also have to demonstrate how the entry requirements and any "bridging" courses offer a sufficient basis for students to proceed satisfactorily on *Fachhochschulen* courses.

There is a very heated debate concerning the relationship between graduates from *Fachhochschulen* and doctoral studies at the university. The universities, for the most part, do not accept the idea that a *Fachhochschule* graduate should be or would be able to enter a doctoral programme directly. We ourselves are not wholly convinced by this view but we recognise the strength of feeling, and the undesirability of forcing what are ultimately academic decisions on the universities. The proposals in the revised draft law appear to offer a reasonable compromise.

However, it is essential that there be a clear articulation of the *Fachhochschulen* with doctoral studies at university. This does not mean that *Fachhochschule* graduates should have automatic entry to these programmes, but entry must be possible through qualifying studies or other means if necessary. We are hopeful that, in time, the universities' experience with *Fachhochschule* graduates will eventually lead them to reconsider their position.

Mixed funding

We have seen that Austria, like other countries, has to consider ways of diversifying the sources of funding for higher education. The proposal to create *Fachhochschulen* relies on the introduction of mixed funding, drawing on funds from provincial authorities, employers and other organisations, and from students themselves through fees.

Our examination has shown that sources other than federal funding are willing to make contributions. Considerable willingness to provide funds to establish institutions has been expressed by provincial authorities and employers. Funds for continuing finance are less easily available, but employers are willing to support individual students through scholarships. The idea of fees for students has been accepted, however reluctantly, by a surprising range of people. *Fachhochschulen* will be offering professional education, where fees are already common.

We would like to emphasize that these proposals should not be understood as an endeavour to privatise higher education. It will remain the duty of the federal government to secure adequate provision of *Fachhochschule* education.

An agenda for implementing the *Fachhochschule* policy

A number of issues will need to be resolved for the implementation of the *Fachhochschule* policy. These constitute a policy agenda for the government – and the institutions – in the coming years.

The functions of the *Fachhochschulen*

There is much debate in Austria about the way in which the *Fachhochschulen* should be differentiated from the universities, and to a lesser extent from the higher vocational sector. The case for a *Fachhochschule* sector rests on the idea that it should offer a different kind of education from the universities, particularly in its vocational emphasis and its shorter duration. This education, on which a consensus will have to be reached, will be different from that currently offered within the higher secondary vocational system. The broad debate we propose on the functions of the whole higher education system would help to offer a framework for establishing this consensus. We offer below some more specific suggestions on the nature of the curriculum for the FHS sector and its links with the secondary sector.

There is also a vexed issue about differentiation in terms of the universities' traditional emphasis on research, particularly "pure" or "basic" research. Strong views are expressed on whether the *Fachhochschulen* should have a research role at all, and how far it should be limited to development, or whether it can be allowed to embrace applied research. This debate can easily become merely semantic and sterile. The distinctions are not, in reality, precise.

It is clear however that there should be some research in *Fachhochschulen,* and that there should be differentiation of emphasis in this research from that in universities. We do not see how those teaching future professionals can do so without experience and understanding of current developments in theory and practice. Equally, we do not believe that this educational purpose would be best achieved if the research concentrated on basic theory. But what is common to education in both sectors is the need for their graduates to have a firm understanding of investigative methods appropriate to their future careers.

This issue perhaps becomes clearer if the "service" function of the *Fachhochschulen* is considered. In addition to offering courses for both initial and continuing education, the *Fachhochschulen* will have an important task of offering advisory and consultancy services to firms of all sizes. This activity is itself investigative; much of their research will arise in this way. Both staff and students may further develop their research skills by undertaking tasks of this sort.

An investment plan

The debate about the draft *Fachhochschule* law has shown the urgent need for a plan for this new sector. Although the *Fachhochschule* policy is an important step towards decentralisation and deregulation, the government has a role to play in determining the overall pattern of provision. Educational provision cannot be entirely left to market mechanisms. The plan should indicate the federal government's general intentions about the size, distribution, proposed growth rates and funding of the sector and the federal government's financial involvement. It would ideally be set in the context of the debate about the functions of the higher education system as a whole that we propose in Chapter 6. It is here that the social partners have a part to play in consideration of the broad purposes of the FHS sector and the distribution of resources. (There is also a role for the federal government as an employer in stating the standards it would seek of FHS graduates in relevant fields. Here, too, the social partners have a legitimate role.)

The investment plan, or some other suitable document, will need to address the extent and nature of the federal government's financial involvement in *Fachhochschulen.* What federal funds will be made available for this sector? What mechanisms will be employed to allocate any such funds to the *Fachhochschulen*? There are suggestions that the government may "purchase' student places from the maintainers of *Fachhochschulen* and that this will be negotiated on a case-by-case basis. If so, it will still need to clarify the basis on which the 'price'' will be determined, and the way in which differential costs, for example between disciplines or localities, will be taken into account. The experience of other OECD countries, such as the United Kingdom, is that such a funding mechanism is complicated and can encourage unexpected responses by institutions.

The plan will need to anticipate the development of the *Fachhochschule* sector in the medium to long term. The revised draft law proposes mechanisms and criteria by which institutions will be able to apply for *Fachhochschule* status. We believe the government needs to have a general view of the future size and shape of the FHS sector for planning purposes, and to relieve the uncertainty expressed by many of our respondents.

The plan should clarify the government's position on the managerial and governance structure it sees as appropriate for institutions in the *Fachhochschule* sector. The government should also resist the pressure to conform to the traditional approach of prescribing in detail the organisational requirements of *Fachhochschulen,* but it could offer a view on the general pattern it expects to see. Does it have a view about the managerial and governance structures that are appropriate for the institutions in this sector? Should there be a governing body of some kind for each institution? How should it be composed in order to properly reflect the interest groups concerned?

Other institutions not meeting all the criteria for FHS status will still be able to offer courses approved by the *Fachhochschulrat,* raising the possibility of a "two-tier" system. This issue also arises in relation to institutions offering courses in non-technological disciplines.

Future sectors to include in the *Fachhochschule*

We believe the government will need to make an early statement, in the investment plan or some other suitable policy document, about the kinds of institutions it intends to bring into the *Fachhochschule* sector in the future. We see a need for an enlargement of the sector as soon as possible, to include education for commerce, business and management, the social academies, paramedical education and pedagogic education. We understand the political and financial difficulties that the inclusion of such institutions raises, and the need for the government to proceed step by step. Most of their graduates are employed in the public sector and their upgrading would be likely to lead to salary increases and an increased burden on public authorities. But these institutions already have some of the features of *Fachhochschulen,* yet may not be included in the *Fachhoch-*

schule sector. We noted that some paramedical colleges, for example, are developing the kinds of curricular ideas about a properly conceived vocational preparation that we advocate below.

There is a substantial educational case for consideration of the extension of the *Fachhochschule* sector. The current proposals are likely to lead to the creation of small, monotechnic institutions. Early consideration should be given to the feasibility of combining related disciplines (such as technology and management) in one institution, for both educational purposes and administrative efficiency. Institutions on more "polytechnic" lines would offer opportunities for cross fertilization of ideas and economies of scale. Furthermore, they would have an adequate resource base at their disposal to offer advisory and consultancy services and the potential for developing a coherent and confident sector of non-university education. This type of institution also offers an important opportunity for equalising the provision of higher education across the country. Regions currently without a university could develop an attractive sector of non-university education, meeting a wide range of needs for both the public and private sectors.

There will be a need to develop such institutions to a comparable quality to the proposed *Fachhochschulen,* steering them away from their school-like ambiance, and towards staff development. One way of proceeding would be for the qualification-awarding bodies to establish similar procedures and criteria for FHS status to those proposed for the *Fachhochschulen* in the draft law.

Curriculum development

We see a need for a consideration of the nature of vocational and professional education at the turn of the 21st century. There is a need for an intellectual framework within which particular courses and curricula would be designed. Much of the current debate is about the particular balance between "theory" and "practice" in courses, rather than about the nature of the courses and the changing demands that students will face in their working lives. The *Fachhochschule* courses cannot just be "more of the same" (an extra year or two added to existing courses) nor watered down university courses (education for drop-outs) but should constitute true vocational higher education.

We have seen examples of innovative thought on this topic from staff in both higher vocational education and the universities in developing courses for proposed *Fachhochschulen.* There is thought, too, in other areas, such as nursing education (for example in the development of "nursing science"). Experience in other OECD countries shows that many professions (particularly in the paramedical field) may move towards graduate status, so developments such as these will need to be extended across the country and to new vocational areas.

There are a number of academic bases for spreading this new thinking. One approach is to develop "profiles" of the cluster of skills, abilities and knowledge that are used by practitioners in each profession (as in Markkula, 1988); this is likely to reveal a greater emphasis on managerial and economic abilities than currently offered in either vocational or university courses. Another interesting approach, discussed in the Background Report, lies in the idea of the "reflective practitioner".

One of the implications of the discussions we have had in Austria is that there may be more than one approach to the curriculum in *Fachhochschulen*. Some have spoken of the need for graduates to be technically expert in their fields, others have emphasized the importance of a combination of skills and knowledge; some have spoken of the need for more general education than is currently offered in BHS courses or the dual system. It would be sensible for the different approaches to be developed and tried, and the outcomes monitored. One of the merits of the *Fachhochschule* system is that variety of courses is possible within strict standards.

Staff development

The successful development of the *Fachhochschule* policy will depend in the long term on the creation of self-confident and self-actuating academic staff. The sector will need to have an independent educational identity, not seen as subordinate to the universities, though different from them. Thus, the staff will need to be capable of initiating change and innovation in response to changing circumstances.

The creation of the new curricula to be offered is fundamental to this, and this initiative will require considerable support for staff development if it is to be undertaken successfully. The proposed "course teams" will be central in curriculum development. They will need to be supported in their work and their achievements will need to be recognised at both institutional and national levels. In this regard, we suggest that further thought may need to be given to the way in which teachers in *Fachhochschulen* are recognised, since the draft law excludes the possibility of a *Fachhochschule* equivalent to the *venia docendi*.

We envisage that the *Fachhochschulen* will require staff from a variety of backgrounds – industry, higher vocational education, university – to provide the expertise needed by a properly conceived vocational education. These staff will need, as we noted earlier, to be able to engage in activities which support the acquisition of experience and understanding of developments in the relevant fields of employment.

The creation of *Fachhochschule* courses will present a challenge to their staff. Whilst we do not wish to denigrate the achievements of staff in existing higher vocational schools, we note that their training in pedagogy is limited; university staff have hitherto designed curricula with ends other than those of the *Fachhochschule* in mind. We have a strong impression that staff have come to accept that most new developments are initiated in the Ministry.

We see a need for the two Education Ministries to undertake early promotion of staff development. The task may at first be simply one of encouraging staff to start thinking about new ideas, rather than developing specific curricula – hence the necessity to start this process before *Fachhochschule* curricula are required. One way may be to enable those who are pioneering new ideas to meet with others in informal discussion groups or seminars. Employers may be persuaded to finance some of these activities.

Staff in *Fachhochschulen* will also, like those in universities, need to be prepared to undertake managerial tasks, since the *Fachhochschulen,* too, will have considerable autonomy.

Implications of the *Fachhochschulen* for secondary education

The introduction of a *Fachhochschule* sector will have implications for secondary education. We believe that this should be managed in a way that enhances the integration of the secondary system.

Austrian education is unusual in the extent and earliness of its selection and in the impermeability between different sectors of secondary education. We see a need in the longer term for reflection on the structure and content of higher secondary education. We believe the government should anticipate that the creation of *Fachhochschulen* will increase the awareness of this need as it raises and addresses questions about the nature of vocational education and its relationship with general education.

In the immediate future, it is likely that the *Fachhochschulen* will lead to the demise of the small *Kollegs* sector which offers vocational courses for graduates from AHS. In the longer term, they may raise questions about the 5th year of higher vocational education. It will be important to ensure that the *Fachhochschulen* do not destroy the five-year BHS route if there is an economic need for it. In any case, it will be important that BHS graduates have the opportunity to obtain a *Fachhochschule* degree through continuing education.

The articulation of the *Fachhochschule* sector with secondary education, and the access routes to *Fachhochschulen* demonstrate the importance of matching the educational profiles of entrants with the curricula in *Fachhochschulen.* The present highly compartmentalised secondary system offers scant opportunity for pupils to redeem earlier decisions; there is little chance of upgrading basic education within the school system. Entry to the first stage of *Fachhochschulen* courses will therefore need to be flexible, to accommodate pupils with different abilities; there could be advanced entry for leavers from the five-year BHS; there could be ''link'' courses for entrants from the dual system. There may be a need for courses in general education to be offered to entrants from these routes (as supplementary professional education may be offered to entrants from AHS).

The question arises of exactly where the distinction between secondary education and *Fachhochschulen* courses is drawn. The *Fachhochschulen* will be able to identify courses in continuing education which they will accept in lieu of *Matura* for some students with vocational experience. If the *Fachhochschulen* offer link or preparatory courses, these will be under the control of the *Fachhochschulrat,* free of direct ministerial regulation and thus more easily matched to the needs of a diverse student population. But the *Fachhochschulen* will not be evenly spread by either geographic or subject area. Similarly, the principle of orderly provision would be violated if the post-secondary *Fachhochschulen* were to offer course at secondary level. The government will need to resolve this dilemma.

Continuing education

Although there is a generally good provision of continuing education in Austria, the focus is on immediate vocational needs. There is a need for a more comprehensive and accessible system of continuing education; the obvious gaps in provision mean that the *Fachhochschulen* could play an important role in this process. It is essential that the rules governing *Fachhochschule* courses set down in the law or the rules of the *Fachhochschulrat* permit these institutions to offer courses in continuing education.

The *Fachhochschulen* could offer courses to upgrade the qualifications of those already in employment (for example, coming from the 5-year BHS), building upon their experiences. Thus, there is a need for part-time as well as full-time education in *Fachhochschulen,* leading in some cases to *Fachhochschule* degrees, with the implications of this for staff development. We note that the draft law allows courses to be offered on a part-time basis.

Consideration could be given to the role that distance education could play in continuing education, especially since *Fachhochschulen* will be limited in number, specialised and hence unevenly distributed across the country. Staff development and curricular development will be needed to support such an innovation. This issue could be included in the plan for the *Fachhochschule* sector. It would be a way of extending the opportunities for innovation in education presented by the *Fachhochschule* policy throughout Austria.

Monitoring

The introduction of the *Fachhochschule* sector is an important experiment in Austrian education, not only in terms of the development of higher education but because it is pioneering a new approach to policy-making and institutional expansion. It is equally important that its progress be monitored and that arrangements for this are put in place as soon as the *Fachhochschule* law is passed. Experience in other countries shows the need to ensure that tendencies such as "academic drift" are detected at an early stage. One of the tasks of the two Ministries and the *Fachhochschulrat* will be to ensure that this takes place. The *Fachhochschulrat* will have a secretariat to support its work, and it will need to ensure that relevant data are collected on the developments in the new sector. It may need to commission external studies to evaluate the outcome of its work periodically. The lessons from monitoring and evaluation will be important, not just for the *Fachhochschule* sector but for the general progress of reform in Austrian education.

Chapter 6

CONCLUSIONS AND RECOMMENDATIONS

This review has tried to set the discussion of current proposals for reform in higher education in Austria in the wider economic, social and political context. We believe that the reform proposals offer a significant opportunity to develop and test some new approaches to policy-making that are important for Austria's future prosperity in changing circumstances. There is more at stake than the introduction of a few new institutions.

The examination starts from the widely acknowledged quality of the products of the Austrian education system, in particular of the graduates from the 5-year BHS courses and university graduates. It is important not to endanger this quality, and we see no reason why the reforms currently proposed should do so.

The system which produces this educational quality is, however, complicated, and widely held to be inefficient in certain respects. Moreover, Austria has to anticipate the need for major changes in its global context.

Our first conclusion therefore is of support for the general thrust of the policies of reform in higher education. Indeed, and in contrast with some of the views expressed to us in Austria, we consider that there is a need for acceleration and broadening of the scope of the reforms.

There are a number of reasons for this conclusion. First, there is a pressing need for change in Austria in response to geopolitical developments, particularly the entry to the EU and the opening of Eastern Europe. Reaching a wider understanding of the implications of these developments will require major adjustments within Austria, not least in educational policy. We see the proposal to introduce a *Fachhochschule* sector as an essential first step in this adjustment, and as introducing a new approach to policy-making in the Austrian context. The proposed reforms of university management are, similarly, a step towards decentralisation and deregulation.

There is a need for some systematisation of the structure of Austrian education. For a small country, its system is at first sight rather heterogeneous, and the tradition of centralisation and regulation means that the system has become compartmentalised. Early and excessive selection, the many routes and levels in secondary education, the few links between them are obvious examples. The "gap" between the age of graduates from higher vocational education (19 years) and those from university (generally 25 to 30) is another example of systematic difficulty, as is the lack of a co-ordinated continuing education system.

We believe that proposals for reform should be set in the context of a principle that the system should be simplified rather than complicated by change, though this is not to say that there should be a *single* solution to any particular curricular or pedagogic issue. The task is to create a plural and responsive, but orderly, system.

In this regard, there is also the problem of geographical imbalance in the pattern of provision of both post-secondary education and the secondary system leading to it. Reforms should help to equalise provision.

A major issue facing all OECD countries is that of financing higher education, particularly as countries move to a mass system of higher education, and most have accepted that it is no longer possible to sustain such a system solely through public funding. Austria faces problems of controlling its budget deficit, and the potential of joining whatever form of monetary system may exist within the EU. It needs to address the widely acknowledged problems of obvious inefficiencies in higher education, student drop-out and the long duration of studies.

All these factors mean that difficult decisions will have to be made in Austria about, *inter alia,* its higher education system. The two reforms we have considered address particular aspects of this problem.

We realise that reform in Austria must take place step by step; proposals for too extensive a change are not politically attainable. But while compromise may be inevitable, it should not be so great that it generates contradictions in the educational policy. The process of reaching an agreement on the progress of university reforms seems particularly vulnerable to this danger. Reform should not be *ad hoc*. The issues of managerial responsibility, curricular reform, effectiveness of the university system and university funding are all interconnected. The controversial issue of student fees, for example, could incite students to complete their studies earlier; it also raises the question of support for students through grants or scholarships. We believe therefore that there is a need for a comprehensive approach to reform of the system. The extent of reform required raises questions about the functions served by higher education in Austria.

The functions of the higher education system

We would like to encourage the government and the higher education system to engage in a broad and public debate about the function, not just of the universities, but of the whole higher education system and the roles of the different kinds of institutions within it. This, in turn, would identify the sequence of steps to be taken in each area to create a more responsive system.

Such a debate would need to consider the balance between the different functions that might be identified for the system as a whole. Such functions might include:

– the education of students for employment;
– the generation of new knowledge;

- the application of knowledge;
- the development of new professional practices;
- the role of higher education as an independent critic of society or government.

The distribution of these functions needs to be considered at four main levels:

- national: the balance of resources allocated to each function in the country as a whole;
- institutional: the balance between these functions in each institution;
- course: the balance between these functions in courses of study;
- individual: the balance between these functions for each member of the academic community.

An agreement about the broad functions of the higher education system would create a clearer context for identifying the role of the universities and of their staffs, and the role of the *Fachhochschulen.*

Reform of the university system

The reforms of university management address the issue of excessive central control and the allocation of reponsibility for decision-making. We see an urgent need for reform in this context. Austrian universities currently have less managerial autonomy than primary schools in some countries. As with other issues in Austria, there is wide agreement on the need for reform, but less on the details, and we detect a need for the university community to establish some consensus here.

The debate on this topic in Austria, as with debate about devolution of education management in other countries, has taken place at a time of financial constraints, and some of the objections to reform confuse the issue of institutional freedom with the level of funding. We believe that universities should have the freedom to manage their budgets whatever the financial circumstances and that they need and should accept the responsibility that this entails.

The government should not, however, underestimate the demands that this places upon the academic community. Experience in other OECD countries confirms that there will be a need for considerable administrative support in the universities if they are to be able to carry out their new responsibilities, and for the training and development of managerial skills in staff whose expertise is often not explicitly in financial or managerial fields.

We do not believe that reform in the universities should be confined to their management. The universities need to recognise the broadly vocational aspirations of most of their students, and the demands of the economy. The complexity and difficulty of central control of university curricula needs to be diminished urgently. There are encouraging initiatives within the universities, but these are often delayed or frustrated by the system of regulation. The universities are not over-inclined to reform and the system enhances this reluctance rather than rewarding initiative and innovation. There is a need to enhance the completion rate of students, and reduce the length of their studies. There is a need to relate the funding of the universities more closely to the functions that they serve. There may be need for even more radical reforms of the functions of academic staff and of their remuneration.

The *Fachhochschulen*

We strongly support the proposal to create *Fachhochschulen.* There is wide agreement within Austria on the need for a new form of post-secondary education through these institutions. There is particularly strong support from employers and others outside the education system; there is also, generally, support for such a sector from the universities. The need for a new kind of education, which would be vocationally oriented and of a duration of approximately three years, is generally accepted.

The draft law to create a *Fachhochschulrat* has generated a number of objections from different sectors of Austrian society and the education system. We believe that the government will be able to accommodate many of the objections to the draft. However, we believe that five essential features of the *Fachhochschule* policy must be retained if it is to be effective:

- *The accreditation model*: the method of accreditation proposed for the *Fachhochschulrat* is a particularly important element of the policy. It offers a way of *deregulating* quality control in Austrian higher education. The *Fachhohchschulen* will be responsible for their own academic development, and will have to demonstrate that their courses meet the general criteria prescribed by the *Fachhochschulrat.* The system eliminates the need for detailed regulation of curricular content and locates reponsibility for *educational* decisions with the *Fachhochschulrat* and the educational institutions.
- *The Fachhochschulrat*: the creation of a separate body for quality control offers a way of *decentralising* this function. We emphasize the limitations of the role of the *Fachhochschulrat.* The responsibility for the national pattern of *Fachhochschule* education has *not* been decentralised. The *Fachhochschulrat* does not decide on which courses will be funded (and it will not approve courses in institutions which cannot demonstrate security of funding). It would be appropriate for it to be broadly composed of people with educational expertise, rather than representative of sectional or political interests.
- *Acceptance of responsibility for student progress*: the *Fachhochschule* policy embodies the principle that the *Fachhochschulen* are responsible for student progress. The task of ensuring that this principle is acknowledged and practised will rest with the *Fachhochschulrat.*
- *Access*: we believe that the *Fachhochschulen* should offer routes to higher education for students from all the different streams in secondary education. They should increase the permeability of the education system, particularly for those who entered the "dual system". There will be a need for different kinds of provision for different students.

Similarly, there must be a clear articulation of the *Fachhochschulen* with doctoral studies at university. This does not mean that *Fachhochschulen* graduates must have automatic entry to these studies, but entry must be possible, through qualifying studies or other means if necessary.

– *Mixed funding*: we believe that Austria, like other countries, has to consider ways of diversifying the sources of funding for higher education. The proposal to create *Fachhochschulen* has demonstrated that there are sources additional to federal funding from provincial authorities, employers and other organisations, and the idea of fees for students has been accepted, however reluctantly, by a surprising range of people.

The implementation of the Fachhochschule policy

There are a number of issues which will need to be resolved for the implementation of the *Fachhochschule* policy. These constitute a policy agenda for the government – and the institutions – in the coming years.

The functions of the Fachhochschulen

There is a need for a statement of the distinct emphasis of the *Fachhochschule* sector, located in relation to the broad functions of higher education identified above. A consensus will need to be reached on the nature of the education offered. This does not mean that *Fachhochschulen* and university education are to be mutually exclusive, and something may be gained from competition between the sectors because the universities may be encouraged to respond to change. Nor should the definition of the differentiation between the sectors be regarded as eternal: its extent may differ according to subject area and it may change from time to time.

We do not see how those teaching future professionals can do so without experience and understanding of current developments in theory and practice, and the government will need to decide how to define the research function of *Fachhochschulen*. The "service" function of the *Fachhochschulen* in offering advice and consultancy to industry heightens this need.

An investment plan

The debate about the draft *Fachhochschule* law has shown the need of a plan for this sector. Government should be responsible for determining the overall pattern of the provision of education which cannot be entirely left to market mechanisms.

The plan should indicate the federal government's general intentions about the size, distribution, proposed growth rates and funding of the sector and federal involvement in funding. The social partners have their part to play in the development plan in consideration of the distribution of scarce resources and the purposes of the sector.

Future sectors to be included in the Fachhochschule

The government should make an early statement of its intentions about the kinds of institutions it intends to bring into the *Fachhochschule* sector in future. We understand the political and financial difficulties that this raises, but some institutions which are already developed along *Fachhochschule* lines may not be included in the sector.

Early consideration should be given to the feasibility of combining related disciplines (such as technology and management) in one institution, for both educational reasons and administrative efficiency.

Curriculum development

The successful development of the *Fachhochschule* policy will depend on the development of self-confident and pro-active academic staff, with an educational philosophy independent of the universities. Curriculum development is a crucial issue and requires fundamentally new thinking. The *Fachhochschule* courses cannot just be "more of the same".

One interesting basis for the development of this new approach lies in the idea of the "reflective practitioner" discussed in the Background Report. There may be more than one approach to the curriculum in *Fachhochschulen*. One of the merits of the *Fachhochschule* system is that a wide variety of courses is possible within strict standards.

Staff development

The *Fachhochschulen* will require staff from a variety of backgrounds – industry, higher vocational education, university – to provide the expertise needed by a properly conceived vocational education in institutions with substantial managerial autonomy. The creation of *Fachhochschule* courses will be a challenge for staff. For this reason the two Ministries of Education should make an early effort to promote staff development.

Implications of the Fachhochschulen for secondary education

The need for a variety of access routes to *Fachhochschulen* demonstrates the importance of matching the educational profiles of entrants with the curricula in *Fachhochschulen*.

The introduction of this new sector will have implications for secondary education. We believe that this should be done in such a way as to enhance the integration of the secondary system. The question arises of exactly where the distinction between secondary education and *Fachhochschulen* courses is drawn. The government will need to resolve the dilemma. We see a need in the longer term for reflection on the structure and content of higher secondary education.

It will be important to ensure that the *Fachhochschulen* do not destroy the five-year BHS route if there is an economic need for it.

Continuing education

The obvious gaps in provision for continuing education in Austria mean that it is essential that the *Fachhochschulen* offer courses in continuing education. Thus, we see a need for part-time as well as full-time education in *Fachhochschulen.*

Consideration could be given to the role that distance education could play in continuing education. This issue could be included in the development plan for the *Fachhochschule* sector. It would be a way of extending the opportunities for educational innovation presented by the *Fachhochschule* policy throughout Austria.

Monitoring

It is essential that the development of the *Fachhochschule* policy be monitored by the government and the *Fachhochschulrat.*

Bibliography

MARKKULA, M. (1988), ''The role and responsibility of the universities in the field of CEE'', in M. Markkula (ed), *Effective Engineering Education,* European Society for Education.

OECD (1988), *Reviews of National Science and Technology Policy: Austria,* OECD, Paris.

OECD (1991), *OECD Economic Surveys: 1990-91: Austria,* OECD, Paris.

OECD (1993), *Education at a Glance – OECD Indicators,* OECD, Paris.

MAIN SALES OUTLETS OF OECD PUBLICATIONS
PRINCIPAUX POINTS DE VENTE DES PUBLICATIONS DE L'OCDE

ARGENTINA – ARGENTINE
Carlos Hirsch S.R.L.
Galería Güemes, Florida 165, 4° Piso
1333 Buenos Aires   Tel. (1) 331.1787 y 331.2391
Telefax: (1) 331.1787

AUSTRALIA – AUSTRALIE
D.A. Information Services
648 Whitehorse Road, P.O.B 163
Mitcham, Victoria 3132   Tel. (03) 873.4411
Telefax: (03) 873.5679

AUSTRIA – AUTRICHE
Gerold & Co.
Graben 31
Wien I   Tel. (0222) 533.50.14
Telefax: (0222) 512.47.31.29

BELGIUM – BELGIQUE
Jean De Lannoy
Avenue du Roi 202
B-1060 Bruxelles   Tel. (02) 538.51.69/538.08.41
Telefax: (02) 538.08.41

CANADA
Renouf Publishing Company Ltd.
1294 Algoma Road
Ottawa, ON K1B 3W8   Tel. (613) 741.4333
Telefax: (613) 741.5439
Stores:
61 Sparks Street
Ottawa, ON K1P 5R1   Tel. (613) 238.8985
211 Yonge Street
Toronto, ON M5B 1M4   Tel. (416) 363.3171
Telefax: (416)363.59.63
Les Éditions La Liberté Inc.
3020 Chemin Sainte-Foy
Sainte-Foy, PQ G1X 3V6   Tel. (418) 658.3763
Telefax: (418) 658.3763
Federal Publications Inc.
165 University Avenue, Suite 701
Toronto, ON M5H 3B8   Tel. (416) 860.1611
Telefax: (416) 860.1608
Les Publications Fédérales
1185 Université
Montréal, QC H3B 3A7   Tel. (514) 954.1633
Telefax: (514) 954.1635

CHINA – CHINE
China National Publications Import
Export Corporation (CNPIEC)
16 Gongti E. Road, Chaoyang District
P.O. Box 88 or 50
Beijing 100704 PR   Tel. (01) 506.6688
Telefax: (01) 506.3101

CHINESE TAIPEI – TAIPEI CHINOIS
Good Faith Worldwide Int'l. Co. Ltd.
9th Floor, No. 118, Sec. 2
Chung Hsiao E. Road
Taipei   Tel. (02) 391.7396/391.7397
Telefax: (02) 394.9176

CZECH REPUBLIC – RÉPUBLIQUE TCHÈQUE
Artia Pegas Press Ltd.
Narodni Trida 25
POB 825
111 21 Praha 1   Tel. 26.65.68
Telefax: 26.20.81

DENMARK – DANEMARK
Munksgaard Book and Subscription Service
35, Nørre Søgade, P.O. Box 2148
DK-1016 København K   Tel. (33) 12.85.70
Telefax: (33) 12.93.87

EGYPT – ÉGYPTE
Middle East Observer
41 Sherif Street
Cairo   Tel. 392.6919
Telefax: 360-6804

FINLAND – FINLANDE
Akateeminen Kirjakauppa
Keskuskatu 1, P.O. Box 128
00100 Helsinki
Subscription Services/Agence d'abonnements :
P.O. Box 23
00371 Helsinki   Tel. (358 0) 12141
Telefax: (358 0) 121.4450

FRANCE
OECD/OCDE
Mail Orders/Commandes par correspondance:
2, rue André-Pascal
75775 Paris Cedex 16   Tel. (33-1) 45.24.82.00
Telefax: (33-1) 49.10.42.76
Telex: 640048 OCDE
Orders via Minitel, France only/
Commandes par Minitel, France exclusivement :
36 15 OCDE
OECD Bookshop/Librairie de l'OCDE :
33, rue Octave-Feuillet
75016 Paris   Tel. (33-1) 45.24.81.81
(33-1) 45.24.81.67
Documentation Française
29, quai Voltaire
75007 Paris   Tel. 40.15.70.00
Gibert Jeune (Droit-Économie)
6, place Saint-Michel
75006 Paris   Tel. 43.25.91.19
Librairie du Commerce International
10, avenue d'Iéna
75016 Paris   Tel. 40.73.34.60
Librairie Dunod
Université Paris-Dauphine
Place du Maréchal de Lattre de Tassigny
75016 Paris   Tel. (1) 44.05.40.13
Librairie Lavoisier
11, rue Lavoisier
75008 Paris   Tel. 42.65.39.95
Librairie L.G.D.J. - Montchrestien
20, rue Soufflot
75005 Paris   Tel. 46.33.89.85
Librairie des Sciences Politiques
30, rue Saint-Guillaume
75007 Paris   Tel. 45.48.36.02
P.U.F.
49, boulevard Saint-Michel
75005 Paris   Tel. 43.25.83.40
Librairie de l'Université
12a, rue Nazareth
13100 Aix-en-Provence   Tel. (16) 42.26.18.08
Documentation Française
165, rue Garibaldi
69003 Lyon   Tel. (16) 78.63.32.23
Librairie Decitre
29, place Bellecour
69002 Lyon   Tel. (16) 72.40.54.54
Librairie Sauramps
Le Triangle
34967 Montpellier Cedex 2 Tel. (16) 67.58.85.15
Tekefax: (16) 67.58.27.36

GERMANY – ALLEMAGNE
OECD Publications and Information Centre
August-Bebel-Allee 6
D-53175 Bonn   Tel. (0228) 959.120
Telefax: (0228) 959.12.17

GREECE – GRÈCE
Librairie Kauffmann
Mavrokordatou 9
106 78 Athens   Tel. (01) 32.55.321
Telefax: (01) 32.30.320

HONG-KONG
Swindon Book Co. Ltd.
Astoria Bldg. 3F
34 Ashley Road, Tsimshatsui
Kowloon, Hong Kong   Tel. 2376.2062
Telefax: 2376.0685

HUNGARY – HONGRIE
Euro Info Service
Margitsziget, Európa Ház
1138 Budapest   Tel. (1) 111.62.16
Telefax: (1) 111.60.61

ICELAND – ISLANDE
Mál Mog Menning
Laugavegi 18, Pósthólf 392
121 Reykjavik   Tel. (1) 552.4240
Telefax: (1) 562.3523

INDIA – INDE
Oxford Book and Stationery Co.
Scindia House
New Delhi 110001   Tel. (11) 331.5896/5308
Telefax: (11) 332.5993
17 Park Street
Calcutta 700016   Tel. 240832

INDONESIA – INDONÉSIE
Pdii-Lipi
P.O. Box 4298
Jakarta 12042   Tel. (21) 573.34.67
Telefax: (21) 573.34.67

IRELAND – IRLANDE
Government Supplies Agency
Publications Section
4/5 Harcourt Road
Dublin 2   Tel. 661.31.11
Telefax: 475.27.60

ISRAEL
Praedicta
5 Shatner Street
P.O. Box 34030
Jerusalem 91430   Tel. (2) 52.84.90/1/2
Telefax: (2) 52.84.93
R.O.Y. International
P.O. Box 13056
Tel Aviv 61130   Tel. (3) 49.61.08
Telefax: (3) 544.60.39
Palestinian Authority/Middle East:
INDEX Information Services
P.O.B. 19502
Jerusalem   Tel. (2) 27.12.19
Telefax: (2) 27.16.34

ITALY – ITALIE
Libreria Commissionaria Sansoni
Via Duca di Calabria 1/1
50125 Firenze   Tel. (055) 64.54.15
Telefax: (055) 64.12.57
Via Bartolini 29
20155 Milano   Tel. (02) 36.50.83
Editrice e Libreria Herder
Piazza Montecitorio 120
00186 Roma   Tel. 679.46.28
Telefax: 678.47.51
Libreria Hoepli
Via Hoepli 5
20121 Milano   Tel. (02) 86.54.46
Telefax: (02) 805.28.86
Libreria Scientifica
Dott. Lucio de Biasio 'Aeiou'
Via Coronelli, 6
20146 Milano   Tel. (02) 48.95.45.52
Telefax: (02) 48.95.45.48

JAPAN – JAPON
OECD Publications and Information Centre
Landic Akasaka Building
2-3-4 Akasaka, Minato-ku
Tokyo 107   Tel. (81.3) 3586.2016
Telefax: (81.3) 3584.7929

KOREA – CORÉE
Kyobo Book Centre Co. Ltd.
P.O. Box 1658, Kwang Hwa Moon
Seoul   Tel. 730.78.91
Telefax: 735.00.30

MALAYSIA – MALAISIE
University of Malaya Bookshop
University of Malaya
P.O. Box 1127, Jalan Pantai Baru
59700 Kuala Lumpur
Malaysia   Tel. 756.5000/756.5425
                            Telefax: 756.3246

MEXICO – MEXIQUE
Revistas y Periodicos Internacionales S.A. de C.V.
Florencia 57 - 1004
Mexico, D.F. 06600   Tel. 207.81.00
                            Telefax: 208.39.79

NETHERLANDS – PAYS-BAS
SDU Uitgeverij Plantijnstraat
Externe Fondsen
Postbus 20014
2500 EA's-Gravenhage   Tel. (070) 37.89.880
Voor bestellingen: Telefax: (070) 34.75.778

NEW ZEALAND
NOUVELLE-ZÉLANDE
Legislation Services
P.O. Box 12418
Thorndon, Wellington   Tel. (04) 496.5652
                           Telefax: (04) 496.5698

NORWAY – NORVÈGE
Narvesen Info Center – NIC
Bertrand Narvesens vei 2
P.O. Box 6125 Etterstad
0602 Oslo 6   Tel. (022) 57.33.00
                          Telefax: (022) 68.19.01

PAKISTAN
Mirza Book Agency
65 Shahrah Quaid-E-Azam
Lahore 54000   Tel. (42) 353.601
                         Telefax: (42) 231.730

PHILIPPINE – PHILIPPINES
International Book Center
5th Floor, Filipinas Life Bldg.
Ayala Avenue
Metro Manila   Tel. 81.96.76
                        Telex 23312 RHP PH

PORTUGAL
Livraria Portugal
Rua do Carmo 70-74
Apart. 2681
1200 Lisboa   Tel. (01) 347.49.82/5
                       Telefax: (01) 347.02.64

SINGAPORE – SINGAPOUR
Gower Asia Pacific Pte Ltd.
Golden Wheel Building
41, Kallang Pudding Road, No. 04-03
Singapore 1334   Tel. 741.5166
                       Telefax: 742.9356

SPAIN – ESPAGNE
Mundi-Prensa Libros S.A.
Castelló 37, Apartado 1223
Madrid 28001   Tel. (91) 431.33.99
                       Telefax: (91) 575.39.98

Libreria Internacional AEDOS
Consejo de Ciento 391
08009 – Barcelona   Tel. (93) 488.30.09
                         Telefax: (93) 487.76.59

Llibreria de la Generalitat
Palau Moja
Rambla dels Estudis, 118
08002 – Barcelona
             (Subscripcions) Tel. (93) 318.80.12
             (Publicacions) Tel. (93) 302.67.23
                         Telefax: (93) 412.18.54

SRI LANKA
Centre for Policy Research
c/o Colombo Agencies Ltd.
No. 300-304, Galle Road
Colombo 3   Tel. (1) 574240, 573551-2
                        Telefax: (1) 575394, 510711

SWEDEN – SUÈDE
Fritzes Customer Service
S–106 47 Stockholm   Tel. (08) 690.90.90
                         Telefax: (08) 20.50.21

Subscription Agency/Agence d'abonnements :
Wennergren-Williams Info AB
P.O. Box 1305
171 25 Solna   Tel. (08) 705.97.50
                        Telefax: (08) 27.00.71

SWITZERLAND – SUISSE
Maditec S.A. (Books and Periodicals - Livres
et périodiques)
Chemin des Palettes 4
Case postale 266
1020 Renens VD 1   Tel. (021) 635.08.65
                       Telefax: (021) 635.07.80

Librairie Payot S.A.
4, place Pépinet
CP 3212
1002 Lausanne   Tel. (021) 341.33.47
                      Telefax: (021) 341.33.45

Librairie Unilivres
6, rue de Candolle
1205 Genève   Tel. (022) 320.26.23
                      Telefax: (022) 329.73.18

Subscription Agency/Agence d'abonnements :
Dynapresse Marketing S.A.
38 avenue Vibert
1227 Carouge   Tel. (022) 308.07.89
                      Telefax: (022) 308.07.99

See also – Voir aussi :
OECD Publications and Information Centre
August-Bebel-Allee 6
D-53175 Bonn (Germany)   Tel. (0228) 959.120
                          Telefax: (0228) 959.12.17

THAILAND – THAÏLANDE
Suksit Siam Co. Ltd.
113, 115 Fuang Nakhon Rd.
Opp. Wat Rajbopith
Bangkok 10200   Tel. (662) 225.9531/2
                          Telefax: (662) 222.5188

TURKEY – TURQUIE
Kültür Yayinlari Is-Türk Ltd. Sti.
Atatürk Bulvari No. 191/Kat 13
Kavaklidere/Ankara   Tel. 428.11.40 Ext. 2458
Dolmabahce Cad. No. 29
Besiktas/Istanbul   Tel. 260.71.88
                             Telex: 43482B

UNITED KINGDOM – ROYAUME-UNI
HMSO
Gen. enquiries   Tel. (071) 873 0011
Postal orders only:
P.O. Box 276, London SW8 5DT
Personal Callers HMSO Bookshop
49 High Holborn, London WC1V 6HB
                          Telefax: (071) 873 8200
Branches at: Belfast, Birmingham, Bristol,
Edinburgh, Manchester

UNITED STATES – ÉTATS-UNIS
OECD Publications and Information Center
2001 L Street N.W., Suite 650
Washington, D.C. 20036-4910 Tel. (202) 785.6323
                            Telefax: (202) 785.0350

VENEZUELA
Libreria del Este
Avda F. Miranda 52, Aptdo. 60337
Edificio Galipán
Caracas 106   Tel. 951.1705/951.2307/951.1297
                       Telegram: Libreste Caracas

Subscription to OECD periodicals may also be
placed through main subscription agencies.

Les abonnements aux publications périodiques de
l'OCDE peuvent être souscrits auprès des
principales agences d'abonnement.

Orders and inquiries from countries where Distribu-
tors have not yet been appointed should be sent to:
OECD Publications Service, 2 rue André-Pascal,
75775 Paris Cedex 16, France.

Les commandes provenant de pays où l'OCDE n'a
pas encore désigné de distributeur peuvent être
adressées à : OCDE, Service des Publications,
2, rue André-Pascal, 75775 Paris Cedex 16, France.

                                         5-1995

OECD PUBLICATIONS, 2 rue André-Pascal, 75775 PARIS CEDEX 16
PRINTED IN FRANCE
(91 95 03 1) ISBN 92-64-14394-7 - No. 47793 1995